All
Access
Sewing

Making your wardrobe work for
you with easy-to-follow projects

Rebecca Cole

All Access Sewing
Copyright © Rebecca Cole 2023

Published by Compass-Publishing UK
ISBN 978-1-915962-27-0

Edited and typeset by The Book Refinery Ltd
www.thebookrefinery.com

Photography © Rebecca Cole
Photo of Rebecca Cole © Thomas Davies, Thomas Byron Photography

A CIP catalogue record for this book is available from the British Library.

Printed and bound by CMP Print, Dorset UK.

This book is dedicated to my girls, Imogen and Milly,
for inspiring me every day to make the world a better place.

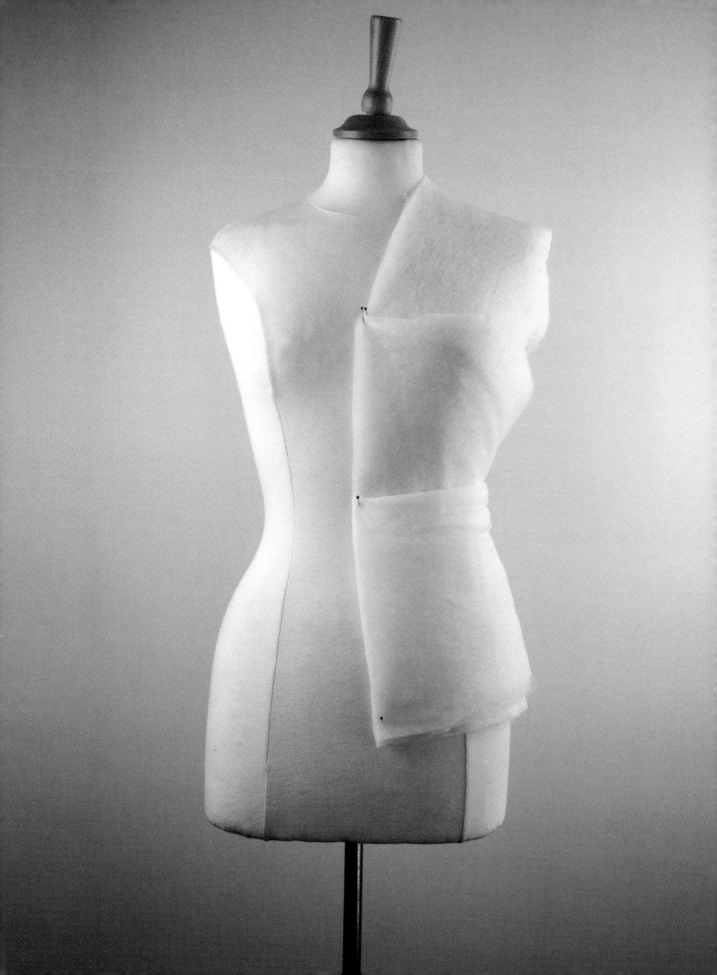

Contents

Foreword

by Victoria Jenkins

The first time I met Becky was over a Zoom call organised by the producers of Channel 4's *Unique Boutique* – although admittedly this was after some emails asking clarifying questions about the designs and fabrics I'd chosen, and what I meant by some of my more erratic sketches.

I was immediately impressed by Becky's boundless knowledge, her passion and her kindness – one of those people I understood and who I felt understood me too.

While we beavered away in the run-up to filming, we spoke almost every day and it wasn't unknown for us to know what the other meant without actually having to say it out loud! That is what Becky has in spades: intuitive knowledge and understanding of a creative problem and the plethora of ways in which it can be fixed, no matter how many seeming obstacles are in the way, whether budget, pattern or machine.

This is what makes her the very best person to be compiling this book: she draws on her own experience and that of many others who work in this space, and writes with empathy, and the understanding that you may never have sewn before and therefore don't need the sometimes scary language that can come from tailors – and, yes, from garment techs like me.

This information deserves to be everywhere so that no one has long years of searching for a solution; no one has to throw away a much-loved garment because it doesn't work for them anymore, when it *could* work, with some tweaks. The reuse, relove, adaptive revolution is here.

I hope this book also shows brands, retailers, tailors, garment professionals etc that they can do so much more and it can have so much impact. Clothes should be made to work with our bodies. We shouldn't be having to force our bodies into clothes that aren't fit for purpose.

I've had sixteen years of experience in the fashion industry and it cannot be overstated how much this book could serve as a lightning rod for change. I'd really lost faith (and still do at times!) that the disabled and chronically sick community would ever be meaningfully included on the high street. Not a single contact I made in those years had time for my ideas with Unhidden.

I still fight now for adaptive fashion to be included but I am definitely held at arm's length. It's a daily campaign for change and, through people like Becky and other incredible adaptive sewers and designers, we are all being the change we want to see. I'm so happy you are reading this and joining us.

Victoria Jenkins

Founder of Unhidden, creators of award-winning adaptive and universal fashion
for people with and without disabilities
Expert Designer on Channel 4's *Unique Boutique*
One of *Vogue*'s top 25 Powerhouse Women defining – and redefining – Britain 2023
One of Vogue Business's top 100 Innovators in Champions For Change category

Introduction

First, let me say WELCOME! I'm so excited you're here – that you have found this book and seen something in it for you. Because this book is for YOU. It is for you and your loved ones; your friends and your family. In fact, the whole premise is that this book is for everyone.

The fashion industry is taking its sweet time to catch on to the idea that not everyone has the same body; that we are all different and varied. Irrespective of the moral implications of ignoring their responsibilities, even the lure of a vastly untapped financial market doesn't seem to be providing a big enough carrot for them to actually make large waves towards changing the status quo. There are a number of people out there working tirelessly to make the changes so desperately needed, but when you're taking on the big names in fashion, it can feel a little David and Goliath.

This book is here to bridge the gap and help us take the control of our wardrobes into our own hands. My aim is to empower everyone to make their clothes work for them. It's what I've been doing with my own clothes over the last couple of years and, oh, my goodness, having a safe and accommodating wardrobe that still reflects my own style and personality makes all the difference.

Sewing for me has been a life-long passion. Growing up, I was the only one of my immediate family who sewed, and I quickly took on the role of fixer and mender. Thankfully, I grew up in the 80s and 90s, when Textiles was still a subject taught in school, and those classes really helped to develop my skills and confidence. The Art and Textiles Department was my happy place, where I could disappear into a world of fabric-based joy.

I suffered a lot of bullying and peer exclusion at school, and sewing actually helped me through some very difficult times as a teenager. It offered a safe island for me in a sea where I just never seemed to belong. Even when I took up the offer of a work place with the BBC in a costume department, which was a dream come true, I always found myself on the outside of the team I worked with. I did make a small handful of dear friends, who are still in my life today, but I'd describe my early working life as clouded by a feeling that I was eternally on the outside of a joke I just didn't get. I have a strong sense of justice and integrity and felt enormous frustration at forever feeling unable to successfully navigate the world of "schmooze" and networking. Although I was extremely good at my job, time and again, those who were able to talk the talk were invited back to film second series and take future jobs, while I was left on the curb, confused as to why I was being sidelined once more.

In 2009, I took the decision to step away from the television industry. I was about to marry my high school sweetheart, Stuart, and I knew I wanted to start a family. I convinced myself this was my reason for walking away. If I had to choose between the two (I didn't, but that's what I told myself), my plans for marriage and children won hands down. However, although I didn't know it at the time, in reality, I was experiencing autistic burnout: the pure, bone-deep exhaustion from trying to fit into a world not designed for me had finally taken its toll.

The relief of being away from the toxic, neurotypical working environment allowed me time to recover and concentrate on growing my family and my dressmaking business, making wedding dresses on my dining room table.

My daughters, Imogen and Amelia, arrived in swift succession but, despite having desperately wanted to be a mother, I did find motherhood incredibly challenging. I used to blame myself for being a terrible mother who just couldn't cope, but I got through the early years with family support and self-reassurances that, as long as my babies knew they were loved, I was doing my best.

Obviously, while my family was so young, I didn't have much time for sewing and, in all honesty, I lost my love of the craft back then. Something quite soul-destroying can occur when you attempt to make money through your creativity. Over years, being forced to defend my charges for putting my skills to use in private commissions became harder and harder and, for the first time in over twenty years, I decided to leave sewing behind. Life was hard and it was no longer the sanctuary it had always been.

It was at this time that Emily came into my life. As did many in their early twenty-teens, I decided my future lay in network marketing. Sewing would no longer be my focus. Emily taught me about this new business and at the same time showed me how to believe in myself. She became a rock in my life and was the first person, outside family, who created a space for me to truly be myself. She remains a steadfast cheerleader in my life today.

The realisation that you can believe in yourself, and that maybe I wasn't the broken, unlovable failure of a human that I'd long ago decided I was, was a pivotal moment in my life. Concluding that network marketing perhaps wasn't the answer to my problems, I took charge of my destiny.

It was actually the Covid lockdown of 2020 that started the ball rolling which led to this book coming to life. During that time, I watched as my daughters struggled with the intense pressure of being locked away from all routine and from the outside world and, after some research and deep soul-searching, I realised I had been raising neurodivergent children. I threw myself headfirst into learning everything I could about autism and ADHD (there really is no bigger sign of autism than the need to absorb all the information about something in as fast a period of time as possible!) and, discovering that they are both highly genetic, I started to examine the wider family for traces of neurodivergence. This soon brought me to the realisation that I, myself, ticked all the same boxes as my girls did.

The dawning realisation that I was autistic and ADHD had the simultaneous effect of being the most wonderful, life-affirming news – and causing the most soul-crushing grief I had ever felt. There is something amazing about finally knowing you aren't broken, you are just wired differently and living in a world not designed for you. But there is also the unpacking of every life moment and memory through this new lens.

However, discovering I was neurodivergent gave me the framework in which, for the first time in thirty-nine years, I was able to start to take control of my life. One of the areas I focused on was the clothes I wore. I had always dressed how I felt others expected me to, irrespective of how uncomfortable the clothes made me feel. Dressing can be challenging for neurodivergent people. Sensory issues aside, with fabrics and fit, there is the executive function involved in selecting an outfit, which can feel thoroughly overwhelming. Flinging open my wardrobe and pulling out all the clothes that didn't feel "safe" was instantly empowering, and I made the decision to use my dressmaking and sewing skills to create and alter clothes to build a capsule wardrobe that did feel "safe".

I documented this journey on social media. Other people with disabilities started to reach out and I began to discover a world outside of the one I had previously known: a world where I felt part of an enormous community.

I learned a huge amount about myself, and how I functioned as a neurodivergent person in the television industry, during the months I was with the BBC *Sewing Bee* team. I also learned to love my neurodivergent self, what to ask for in a working environment, and how to advocate for myself.

However, it was Channel 4's *Unique Boutique* which was the first working environment where I felt I could be my complete and true self. I was appointed as the Sewing Producer and the team was a highly diverse mix of disabled and neurodivergent people, with everyone being accommodated and included. It was a beautiful experience to be in a working environment with such a dynamic. The people I came into contact with throughout the show inspired me in every way and I was able to use my skills of adaptation in working with the garments created. The joy of full acceptance I experienced has left me feeling renewed in confidence in who I am and what I can bring to the world. *All Access Sewing* was born from this mindset.

There is a group of incredible people working tirelessly to petition the fashion industry and bring adaptive fashion to the world. And shows like *Unique Boutique* bring awareness and begin important conversations. However, nowhere is there a resource to bridge the gap and empower people to take control of their own fashion and clothes. No one is showing how to make sewing accessible to everyone. I am incredibly passionate about the future of accessibility and the role *All Access Sewing* will play within it.

So, here is my invitation to you to come on this journey with me. Yes, the fashion industry needs to wake up and act. But in the meantime, let's make our wardrobes work for us. We are in charge here!

DISCLAIMER

I want this book to be for everyone. To have everyone represented and catered for. However, the human experience is infinitely varied, as are the different bodies we live in. I am a (mostly) cis white woman who, apart from having a brain that functions differently (autism, ADHD and Irlen Syndrome) and a thyroid that is on a permanent vacation, I'm aware I am writing from a place of privilege. I cannot, and will not, appropriate another person's experience of disability. Therefore, I have invited other disabled sewers to share their experiences with us in this book. I want the book to be a community voice. I've worked very hard to make sure as many people are represented here as possible, but I know there will be people who don't see themselves in these pages. And I can only apologise for that. However, please be patient with me. I hope this book will be the start of a revolution in sewing and crafting. It's an ever-moving, growing and changing concept that will evolve over time to become even more inclusive, and I will continue working towards this end.

The projects in the book are open to all to use to make their wardrobes more suitable to their needs. You don't need to be disabled to use this book. Accessibility isn't about making an environment suitable for the disabled community; it's about making an environment work for everybody, the disabled included – just as a ramp allows EVERYBODY entry into a building. That is true accessibility. And that is the whole concept of this book.

WHO IS THIS BOOK FOR?

This is a sewing book with a difference. The idea is to demonstrate how to take items you already own, or have found in traditional shops or online, and adapt them to meet your or a loved one's needs. The projects are all suitable for the adventurous beginner, with clear images and instructions. However, this isn't a beginner's how-to book; I am not taking you through the specifics of beginner sewing. There's a plethora of information available online on how to insert a zip, for example. The projects in this book are about how to use that skill in a way that makes our clothing more accessible, and to inspire a revolution in adapting our own fashion items. Each project is suitable for several different access situations and can be beneficial to everyone, disabled or not.

My main goal with this book is to inspire. For every person out there who has dreamed of taking up sewing but has been held back, either by their own limiting beliefs or for fear that a physical disability would make it impossible; and for every person who has experienced a health challenge or acquired a disability during their lifetime and would love to revisit the hobby they felt they had to say goodbye to – I want this book to remind them that they can come back to sewing. And if you have always sewn, this book is an introduction to how to use those skills to adapt clothing for yourself, loved ones, or even to start a business altering clothing for those who can't do it for themselves.

WHAT IS COVERED?

The book is made up of three sections. First, we show you how to set up your sewing room and put together your sewing kit. There is a wealth of advice and tips from different disabled sewers included within these pages, together with clear images and information on some great sewing-tool initiatives that can help make sewing a more accessible craft.

Secondly, you will meet several different sewers, all of whom work with various disabilities. They share their stories and experiences to help inspire you to get sewing and prove that you can do it too!

Lastly, there are fifteen projects, all designed to help you adapt your own wardrobe, simply and easily, to create clothing that works for you and your body. Each project is designed to work for everyone regardless of your specific needs, so pick and choose the ones that inspire you the most.

HOW TO USE THE BOOK

My aim has been to make this book as clear and accessible as possible. Ease of use has been key. The typeface and layouts have been specifically chosen with this in mind.

The projects are easily accessible. I have split them into three categories: ACCESS, ADJUST and COMFORT. These categories are clearly indicated with differing colours to make each one easily distinguishable. I have decided not to include timings in the project guides, as everyone will work at different rates depending on ability and circumstances. However, I have included guides on how fiddly a project might be and the amount of heavy lifting involved to help inform you of the energy levels and dexterity requirements for each project. These are indicated by a box, found at the beginning of each project.

I also give an indicator of how challenging a project is for the beginners out there.

 Fiddly / dexterity requirements

 Heavy lifting / energy requirements

 Difficulty

Please bear in mind that the projects in the book are designed to be used on existing clothing. All clothing is made slightly differently, so please be flexible when approaching them. I've used garments in the projects that have been constructed in traditional ways so it's easy to follow and apply the techniques to your own garments.

THE GLOSSARY

The Glossary at the back is to explain certain sewing terms, so again, whether you've sewn all your life or have never before picked up a needle, this book is for you.

However this book serves you, I hope you enjoy working with it. I most definitely consider myself and my work a project in progress, but as long as we're taking steps forwards, we're moving in the right direction.

Getting Set Up

Your Sewing Space & Equipment

ARRANGING YOUR SEWING SPACE

Creating a sewing space that works for you is vitally important when it comes to making sewing accessible. Everyone will have different access needs and space requirements. Some may be able to dedicate an entire room in their home to sewing; others may be confined to their dining-room table. Whatever your situation, taking some time to assess how you need your space to serve you is the key to creating a working sewing space.

Things to consider when setting up your sewing space:

WHAT DO YOU WANT TO MAKE?

The genre of sewing you choose to focus on will inform how you set up your space. Dressmaking, large quilts, and curtains, for example, will use larger amounts of fabric, so will mean you'll need a larger work area, either on a table or the floor.

Bag making, cushions, lap quilts, soft toys, or doing alterations to and upcycling clothes will require a smaller work area as they require less space.

WORK SURFACE

» Where will you be setting up your sewing machine or cutting out your fabric? On a specially designed sewing table, on your dining-room table, on the floor, or somewhere else?

» Will you be able to leave your sewing machine and projects out all the time or will you need to pack everything away at the end of the day?

» How does this fit with your energy levels?

» Consider the height of your work surface. Will you be standing to cut and/or sew?

» Will you be seated or will you need space for a wheelchair?

» Do you need the height of your work surface to be adjustable?

MOBILITY

» How easy do you find it to move around from one place to another?

» Do you need to have everything in one place so you can stay as stationary as possible, or are you able to spread out and move between areas?

SEATING

Where you sit in your sewing space is very important.

» Are you a wheelchair user requiring space for your wheelchair at your work desk?

» If you have mobility challenges, would a wheeled chair work best?

» Are you able to have a comfortable cushion and will your back be supported?

» Are you able to reach the foot pedal if needed?

» Sitting at a sewing machine for long periods of time can be very bad for the posture, so make sure you choose seating that supports you in all the ways you need.

LIGHTING

» Lighting is very important when you are sewing. If you're working in a dark space without much natural light, consider what lighting you will use to illuminate your work space.

» Using daylight bulbs in lamps and in your sewing machine will help to reduce eye strain.

» If you experience Visual Stress, Irlen Syndrome, or have sensory issues around light, what colour light would work best for you?

» If you have dexterity challenges, would a touch lamp be a worthwhile investment?

SEWING KIT

Having your sewing kit easily accessible will be paramount for every sewer, irrespective of access needs. As you sew, you will require easy access to the equipment and tools that allow you to do the job. What will work best for you?

» A sewing caddy or box that stays in one place next to you and doesn't get moved from place to place?

ARRANGING YOUR SEWING SPACE

» A mobile sewing kit on a wheeled trolley that can be moved around easily with you, or stored away at the end of the day?

» Multiple sewing kits so you always have access to what you need wherever you are in your space?

» A sewing bag that attaches to a wheelchair?

» Everything in a set place on a peg board on the wall, so you can easily keep track of where it all is?

Choosing your sewing machine

There are a virtually limitless number of different types of sewing machine out there to pick from: sewing machines, overlockers, cover stitch machines, embroidery machines, industrial sewing machines, long arm quilting machines, cutting machines … For every sewing need, there is a machine out there to serve it.

Probably the most important decision you'll make on your sewing journey is what sewing machine to use. There have been numerous developments in sewing machine technology, all of which serve to make sewing easier, more comfortable and also more accessible.

ACCESSIBLE SEWING MACHINE FEATURES:

» **Computerised** – mechanical sewing machines, although they still do the job, aren't as accessible as computerised sewing machines. All the term "computerised" means is that there is an intelligence built into the machine that does all the hard work for you, similar to the way computers now run our cars. When I first learned to sew in the late 80s, early 90s, there was a whole "language" I needed to learn and, back then, there was no access to the internet for guidance. Nowadays, a computerised sewing machine is generally easier to understand and use, safer, more comfortable, and removes a lot of the necessity to learn the jargon of sewing machines.

Computerised sewing machine

» **Stop-start button** – a stop-start button is imperative for anyone wanting to use a sewing machine, who isn't able to access a foot pedal. This could be because they don't have use of their legs or have a lower limb difference; because they are sewing from bed; maybe their only work surface is higher off the ground than a foot pedal can reach, for example, a breakfast bar; or maybe their feet don't reach the foot pedal if they're of shorter stature. From an accessibility point of view, the stop-start button is the greatest development in sewing machine technology, in my opinion.

» **Speed limiter** – a speed limiter on a sewing machine enables the user to control the speed of the machine. If you are a beginner, or working on something delicate or intricate, you may benefit from being able to reduce the maximum speed of the machine. Similarly, if you find controlling the speed with a foot pedal challenging for any reason, limiting the maximum speed can help with this. Another reason I recommend a speed limiter on your machine is that, if for any reason you have to change from sewing with a foot pedal to sewing using a stop-start button, this can take a little time to adjust to. Slowing the speed of the machine will give you greater thinking time while you adapt to this different way of sewing.

» **Thread cutter button** – an automatic thread cutter button will cut the threads automatically, removing the necessity to cut them manually at the end of sewing. Any half-decent machine will have thread cutters built into the sides, which are also handy, but these still involve the fabric being pulled from the machine and the threads cut manually. An automatic thread cutter button will remove this step, helping to reduce fatigue, dexterity requirements, and making the sewing job quicker and more efficient if maintaining attention is your challenge.

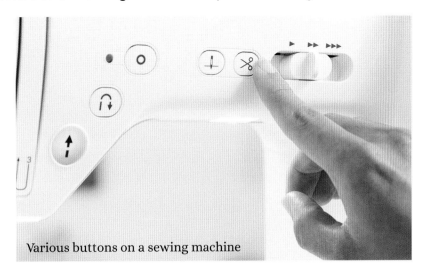

Various buttons on a sewing machine

» **Automatic needle threader** – an automatic needle threader will thread your machine needle for you, removing the need for dexterity and keen vision to do this by hand. Different machines will have different types of automatic needle threader – some are more involved than others – so select a machine that works well for you.

» **Alerts and alarms** – a computerised sewing machine will come packed with alerts and alarms that will let you know when something isn't right, or if some action needs to be taken. At the lowest end of the scale, these sounds will alert you with an error message if something is preventing the machine from working – for example, if the presser foot hasn't been lowered, or if the needle has hit something it can't penetrate and caused a jam*. A slightly more advanced sewing machine may have bobbin and top thread alarms to alert you that the bobbin needs refilling or the top thread has snapped. All these alerts help with safe use of a sewing machine.

» **Knee lift** – a knee lift is quite possibly my favourite addition to a sewing machine. It's a mechanism that heralds from industrial sewing machines, which enables the sewer to control the raising and lowering of the presser foot with their knee, leaving their hands free to hold the fabric being sewn. Knee lifts are great if you have difficulty using a foot pedal but still have use of your legs. They also help if you have an upper body limb difference, as there is less to control with the hands. A knee lift assists too when positioning fabric under the presser foot, as it can be controlled without needing to move your hands from the fabric.

Knee lift

---

* Something I always remind people is that needles are a consumable in sewing. They are designed to be replaced (every eight hours of sewing), and to break if something goes wrong. This is to protect the sewing machine from being damaged, so don't worry if your needle breaks!

Additional sewing machines

The stage you are at on your sewing journey will most likely dictate how many different types of sewing machine you use. If you are just starting out, or have limited space, you may only wish to have a standard sewing machine. However, at some point, you might like to add an overlocker to your collection, if you haven't already. Overlockers are incredibly useful machines for creating professional-looking, finished seams, and for sewing up stretch fabrics, such as jersey. They are, however, traditionally not very accessible sewing machines, being notoriously hard to thread, even without access challenges. Although the newer models are now mostly being fitted with automatic needle threaders, they have yet to be designed with a stop-start button control, so currently rely on the use of a foot pedal. I hope this will be adapted in the near future but, at the time of writing, it's not something that exists on the market.

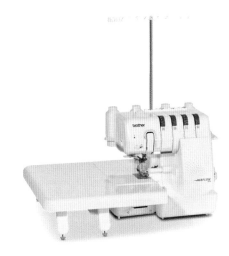

Overlocker

A new development in overlockers that has helped make them more accessible is the invention of the air threader overlocker. An air threader overlocker uses puffs of air to force the thread through the machine to thread it up, making it much easier to use. As this technology is still relatively new, an air threader overlocker is a more expensive investment than a traditional overlocker. However, I believe the hugely improved accessibility is worth the investment, if you are able.

Pressing station

After your sewing machine, your iron and ironing board set-up will be the next most important part of your sewing room, both for achieving professional-looking results and for making your space accessible. There are a number of options available.

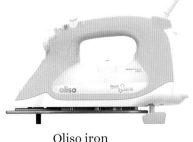

Oliso iron

>> Oliso iron – the Oliso iron is a great advance in technology and very accessible. It's more expensive than more basic irons on the market but, if your budget allows, I believe it's worth the investment. The Oliso iron lifts and lowers

ARRANGING YOUR SEWING SPACE

itself from the surface of the ironing board at the touch of the handle. This means it doesn't need to be placed on and lifted off the fabric. Once you remove your hand from the handle, it lifts itself up, without the fabric being scorched. This also gives it a lower centre of gravity, making it harder to knock over and thus safer to use.

» Ironing mat – if a traditional ironing board is inaccessible for you – for example, if your space doesn't allow for it, or standing for long periods isn't possible – an ironing mat may be a good solution. This is a heat-proof fabric mat that can be folded up and put away when not in use. It can be used on a table or on the floor, wherever is most convenient for you. (1)

» Silicone iron stand – if your budget doesn't allow for the Oliso iron but you find lifting irons a challenge, a silicone iron stand may be the answer. The silicone is heat proof allowing the iron to be kept flat when not in use. This removes the need to continually raise the iron to an upright position. (2)

» Small craft iron – a small craft iron, such as this one by Prym, can be a good accessible option for your pressing. It's light, and easy to store and manoeuvre. (3)

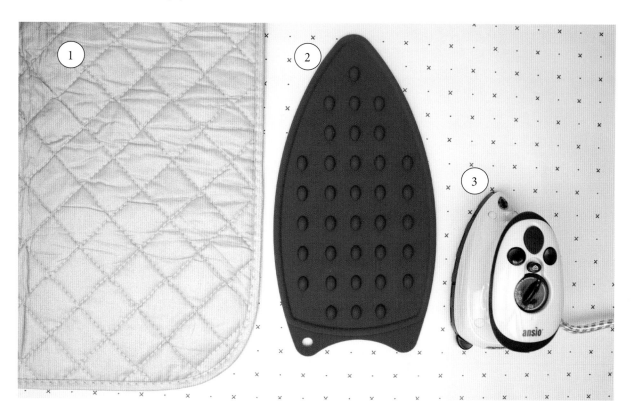

Dress forms

If you are looking to make or adapt clothing, a dress form is a great addition to your sewing space. These are formed shapes that echo the human body and can be used to drape fabric onto or test the fit of something. Unfortunately, there are few forms that represent the disabled body, so some adjustment can be required. Bear in mind, also, whether the stand for your dress form emerges from the leg (meaning it can accommodate crotched garments, such as trousers, shorts or underwear) or from the centre (meaning it will be unable to accommodate crotched garments).

THERE ARE TWO MAIN TYPES OF DRESS FORM:

» **Formed dress form** – these are generally made from a formed polystyrene shape covered in a stretchy fabric sheath. The best way to reshape a formed dress form is to pad it out with wadding. That way you can adapt the shape and size to better suit your own needs. These dress forms can be easily pinned into. (1)

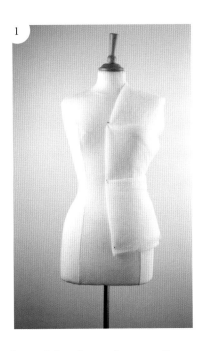 

» **Adjustable dress form** – these are usually hollow carbon fibre forms covered in a felt-like fabric that sits on an adjustable metal framework. There are normally dials at the waist, hips and bust, at four points around the

ARRANGING YOUR SEWING SPACE

body – front, left side, back and right side. These dials are numbered and correspond to individual measurements, meaning they can be adjusted to match bust, waist and hip sizes. However, these dress forms aren't so easy to pin into. (2)

Whatever your space or situation, setting yourself up to sew can feel daunting. No doubt you won't have all the answers immediately; it will definitely be a case of trial and error while you discover what does and doesn't work for you. The main thing is to make a start. Begin with the essentials and work your way up from there. You'll soon learn what you need. A sewing space is a highly personal set-up and what works for someone else may not work for you. But as long as you have a sewing machine and a basic kit, you can get started.

Top Tip!

It can take time to set up a sewing space. Don't feel you have to do everything at once or get it right first time. The most important thing to remember is that your sewing space should make you feel happy! Sewing should bring joy, so make your space your own. By using your space you will also discover problems and solutions that you may not have realised at first.

SEWING ROOM EQUIPMENT

The tools and equipment you have in your sewing kit can make all the difference to accessing sewing. Ideally, you want sewing equipment that supports and assists you, while also being pleasurable and convenient to use. Traditional sewing tools are great but they can sometimes hinder rather than support the disabled or neurodivergent sewer. Thankfully, nowadays, there are far more options available.

Here are some suggestions for items that can be included in your kit to aid you on your sewing journey.

Cutting

1. ELECTRIC SCISSORS

Battery-powered scissors that cut through fabric with no effort! These are very fast and relatively heavy to use, but great if using traditional shears is a challenge.

2. ROTARY CUTTERS

Rotary cutters cut fabric using a circular blade that is rolled along the fabric cutting line. These must be used with a cutting mat or they will damage your work surface. They are helpful as they require less effort to use than shears, but can make cutting out small curves a challenge. They come in all shapes and sizes. The one pictured is a symmetrical handled cutter with a pinking blade attached.

3. SPRING-LOADED SHEARS

Traditional fabric-cutting shears but with the added bonus that the handles are spring-loaded, meaning the hands are only doing half the work. This can help reduce hand fatigue.

4. DUCKBILL SCISSORS

These scissors make light work of trimming down French seams – great for when you're creating sensory-friendly seams. They can also reduce the risk of slipping and snipping a part of a seam you don't want to cut, meaning they are fantastic for unsteady hands.

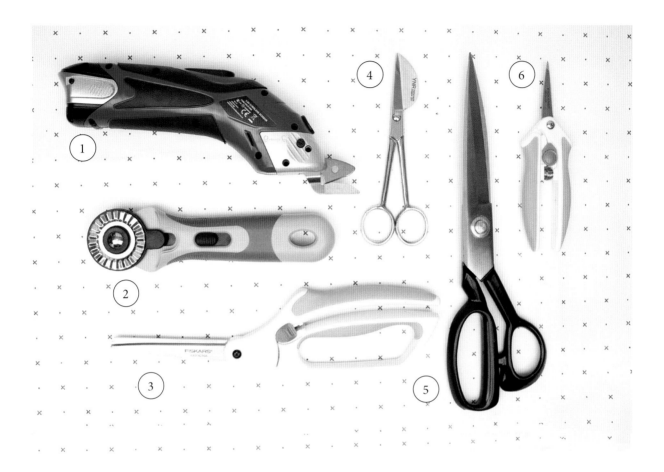

5. FABRIC SHEARS

Traditional fabric shears can be quite heavy and usually have long blades, making them a potential challenge for anyone experiencing hand fatigue or dexterity issues. However, for the sewer who prefers some weight behind their shears, a long-bladed, sharp pair of shears will make light work of any fabric and, for those so inclined, will feel beautiful to wield.

6. SPRING-LOADED SNIPS

These work in a similar way to the spring-loaded shears. They are useful for smaller, more intricate work. Ergonomic handles make them comfortable for the hand, while the spring-loaded action can help reduce hand fatigue.

SEWING ROOM EQUIPMENT

Tools

1. RULER HANDLE

Rulers are a great addition to your sewing kit, whether you are dressmaking, quilting, bag making, or doing any other form of sewing. However, they can be challenging to handle because they lie flat to the work surface. Ruler handles are most commonly handles with rubber suction pads that stick to the ruler, providing a handle for lifting and moving the ruler around.

2. COLOUR-CODED TAPE MEASURE

A tape measure is a must-have item in a sewing kit. It's a flexible tape, with numbers as on a ruler, used for measuring. Most come with both metric and imperial measurements. The tape measure pictured uses different colours to differentiate 10cm blocks, making it easier to keep track of the numbers when measuring.

3. RETRACTABLE TAPE MEASURE

A traditional tape measure that retracts inside a case at the press of a button. This is handy for reducing the amount of storage space your tape measure takes up, but also means the tape is not a trip hazard and won't get caught in chair wheels while you're using it.

4. LOOP TURNER

Loop turners are tools for turning through fabric tubes – often used for bag straps, rouleaux loops, waist ties and so on. Turning through fabric loops is both fiddly and time consuming. Using loop turners makes the process quick and easy, and requires much less dexterity.

5. NOTCH CUTTERS

Notches are marks used to line up pattern pieces and are traditionally created by snipping small cuts into fabric where a pattern piece indicates a notch with a triangle symbol. This can be a fiddly task requiring a steady hand. Notch cutters cut the notch into the fabric with the same motion that's required to use a pair of pliers or snips, making them much easier to handle than scissors. They are also very satisfying to use!

6. TABLE-MOUNTED STITCH RIPPER

A stitch ripper that secures to a work surface with a suction cup at the base. This leaves both hands free to handle the fabric when opening up a seam.

7. ADJUSTABLE THIMBLE

Thimbles are great for protecting the fingertips during sewing, especially if you experience numbness or have sensitive skin. They can also be used to help push straight pins and needles through fabric, reducing the need to pull the needles or pins all the way through the fabric with your fingers. An adjustable thimble doesn't cover the whole finger tip and can be adjusted to fit perfectly. If you experience swelling in your hands, the size can be adapted to suit your needs on a day-to-day basis.

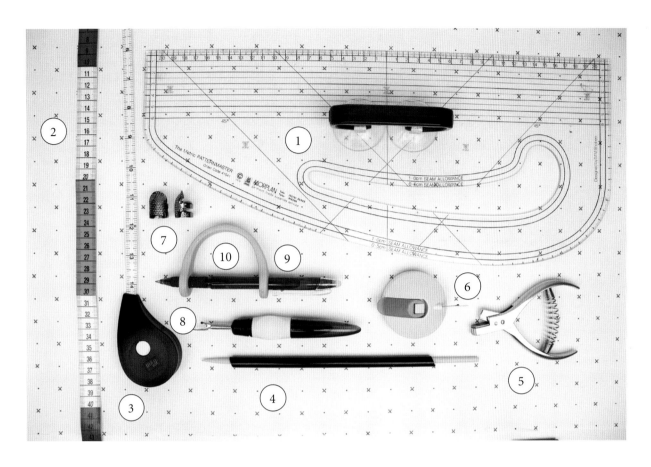

8. ERGONOMIC STITCH RIPPER

A traditional, hand-held stitch ripper with an ergonomic handle, which allows for easier grip and control when unpicking seams or stitches.

9. ERASABLE FABRIC MARKER PENS

Erasable fabric markers are great for using on fabric, as the ink stays put where you mark with it but will disappear when heat is applied, or the eraser on the pen end is used. They are useful for marking seam lines and points on fabric impermanently, with precision and ease. They can permanently mark some fabrics, however, so make sure you test on an inconspicuous area or scrap sample first.

10. EASI-HOLD SILICONE STRAPS

These silicone straps are a great accessibility tool in day-to-day life, as they provide support in gripping everyday items such as cutlery or a toothbrush. They can also be a fantastic addition to a sewing kit for use with many tools, such as fabric pens, chalk pencils, stitch rippers and so on. They come in various sizes and with differing sized holes at the ends, allowing for different implements to be held.

SEWING ROOM EQUIPMENT

11. RUBBER FINGER GRIPS

Traditionally used in schools to help children hold pencils, these are also a helpful addition to a sewing kit to assist with holding markers, such as fabric pens and chalk pencils. They simply slide on to the pen or pencil and provide a shape that's easy to hold. They come in various different styles so there's plenty of choice when it comes to finding what works for you.

12. CHACO LINER PEN

These chalk pens use a small, spiked roller disc in the tip to distribute chalk powder in a straight line. Whereas traditional tailor's chalk can be imprecise and feel unpleasant in the hands if you have sensory issues, a Chaco pen uses chalk in a similar way but with much more accurate results, and it's more sensory friendly. You can also purchase refills when the chalk runs out.

13. SEWER'S THIRD FINGER

This tool is great when you wish you had an extra pair of hands to hold your project. The prongs can be used to hold down seams while pressing, helping to avoid burning fingers with the ironing plate or steam. The tool can also be used to help guide fabric under a sewing machine presser foot, keeping hands and fingers away from the mechanism of a moving sewing needle.

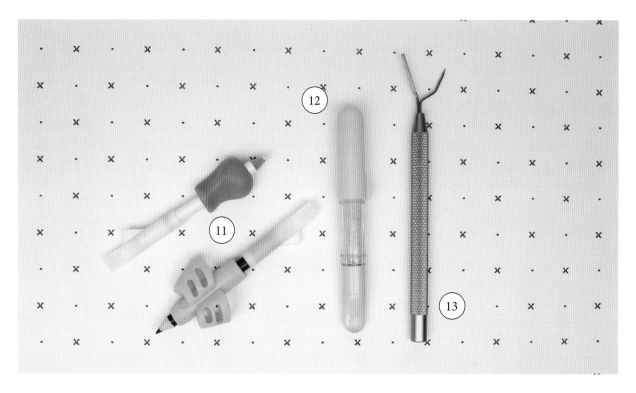

Pinning and threading

1. PIN MAGNET

A pin magnet is a brilliant accessible tool for storing your straight pins, but this one from Zirkel wins hands down. It contains a clever magnet, which means the pins are automatically stored with heads pointing outwards. This makes retrieving your pins so much easier – and safer!

2. EASY GRIP STRAIGHT PINS

Gripping a pin head can be challenging at the best of times. Add in dexterity or fatigue challenges and it can be a real stumbling block to accessing sewing. Using easy grip straight pins with larger heads can make all the difference when working with straight pins.

3. CURVED SAFETY PINS

Curved safety pins are designed for use in quilting but they can actually be used for any sewing project. Their shape means the pin feeds back through to the front of the fabric more easily, making these pins great for reducing the effort required to use them.

4. SELF-THREADING NEEDLES

Anyone who has ever attempted to thread a hand sewing needle will testify to the challenge this can present. The dexterity and clear, close vision required is immense. Self-threading needles are designed with an opening at the top of the eye. This means the thread can be slotted into the eye through this slit, making threading much easier and requiring far less dexterity.

5. FABRIC CLIPS

Fabric clips are small clamps that can be used in the place of straight pins to hold fabric together while you sew. They are very easy to use and can be a highly effective accessible alternative to straight pins. The only downside is that they cannot be used to hold fabric when the edges aren't free – for example when positioning patch pockets. If straight pins aren't an option for you, then fabric glue is a great alternative in situations like this.

6. NEEDLE PULLER

This gadget is designed to make light work of gripping and pulling straight pins and sewing needles through fabric. It clamps on to the pin, making it easier to pull out. It also doubles up as a thimble and thread cutter, so three in one with this one!

7. SEWING MACHINE NEEDLE THREADER

If you don't have access to a sewing machine with a built-in needle threader, this handy gadget can take its place. It's designed to push the thread through the eye of the machine needle, and has a handy hook to grab the loop the other side and pull it through the rest of the way.

SEWING KIT

8 HAND SEWING NEEDLE THREADER

This is such a useful piece of kit. You insert the head end of the sewing needle into the tube at the top. The thread is placed in a groove on the body of the needle threader and a press of a lever pushes the thread through the eye of the needle. It makes seriously light work of threading those hand sewing needles.

9. TEXTILE GLUE STICK

Much like many other craft glues, this comes in a recognisable stick form but is for use specifically with fabric. This glue is a temporary adhesive that won't gunk up your sewing needle and is great for holding sewing projects together in place of straight pins or fabric clips. For example, it's fantastic for anchoring zips or patch pockets, ready for sewing.

10. TRADITIONAL NEEDLE THREADER

A traditional needle threader is made up of a diamond-shaped loop of wire attached to a thin metal disk. This can be just as fiddly to use as threading a needle by hand. However, although the version pictured is based on the same design, it has some accessible features added. The handle is a chunkier shape, making it easier to grip, and the loop of wire sits in front of a dark metal extension. The wire loop is much easier to see against the dark metal, and the metal also provides a rest for the needle, reducing the dexterity required to use the threader.

11. PATTERN WEIGHTS

Pattern weights are a great tool for holding pattern pieces in place while they are being cut out, usually in conjunction with a rotary cutter. Heavier weights reduce the chance of the pattern pieces slipping while being cut. Pattern weights come in all shapes and sizes, often as rice or bead-filled fabric bags. Those pictured are heavy-weight washers, which can be found in any DIY store, and they create much heavier versions, making them effective to use as pattern weights.

12. TEMPORARY BASTING SPRAY

This temporary glue-based spray can be used to stick fabric together for sewing or cutting, without gunking up your sewing needle. It's especially useful for holding large fabric panels or paper pattern pieces in place for cutting or sewing.

Top Tip!

A sewing kit is a very personal thing. While one person will love one type of scissors, another will much prefer a rotary cutter. Only select the tools that work for you and that you enjoy using.

Interviews
&
Projects

Yvonne Coleclough

Yvonne has sewn since she was a child, always making her own clothes. A diagnosis of multiple sclerosis (MS) left her feeling she would have to give up her beloved hobby. However, with some determination, and a helping hand from her husband, she managed to find her way back to it and now loves to sew even more.

"Being disabled doesn't mean you've got to stop what you love or that you can't start to learn, because there are always ways around any challenges. It's not always easy or perfect, but you can still really enjoy it."

HOW DID YOU GET INTO SEWING?

No one at home in our family sewed but I really wanted to learn. A family friend was a very talented sewer and, after I requested help, gave me some sewing lessons. This started the bug and I was hooked. I had sewing lessons at school and absolutely loved them. I've been sewing since I was about seven years old and it's been a part of my life ever since.

I would sew my own clothes and even made my sister's wedding dress!

After I was given my diagnosis, I didn't think I'd be able to sew anymore because I was too unwell. And there was a period of time when this was the case. However, once I was no longer able to work, I returned to sewing to keep myself busy. Not only did I find I was able to sew again, with a few adjustments to accommodate my new

normal, but it actually became my therapy. I don't think I'm overstating it when I say that sewing saved my life. At a time when my whole world had been turned upside down, sewing helped me combat my depression and gave me back a sense of purpose. The sewing community has always been so lovely and supportive, ready to share advice and guidance. Being part of something so inclusive and wonderful has helped me hugely.

WHAT CHALLENGES HAVE YOU FOUND WITH ACCESSING THE CRAFT?

My main challenge with sewing now is managing my fatigue. I can be feeling really great and then, ten minutes into a project, I can hit a wall of deep fatigue, which means my body and brain just shut down and I can't do anymore. I've found ways to try to manage this – the main one is to be really strict with myself about where I spend my energy, and to pace myself. I'm not always successful with this but I do understand it's what I have to do or I can make my symptoms worse.

I'm lucky in that my husband helps me a great deal. I appreciate that not everyone will have somebody who's willing to help them as my husband does, but I do feel, even if I didn't have his help, I could find a way to make it work. However, having his support does make a huge difference, because it gives me a choice as to where I spend my energy. For example, I try not to do any of my own cutting-out. My hands don't work all that well and I would definitely struggle to get on the floor. If I did cut out my fabric pieces, it could make me so poorly it would take me a week to recover and I wouldn't be able to sew. I've learned to pick my battles with where I spend my energy, so I choose to ask for help with this step. This way I can balance out what I can do with what I find more challenging, which, for me, works really well. The thing I find hardest about managing my energy levels is making sure I don't spend too long sewing at any one time. On a good day, I'm always tempted to just keep going because, in my body and mind at that time, I feel I can. However, when I've done this in the past – when I've pushed through, convincing myself I'll be fine – invariably I wake up the next day and find I can't move. This is very frustrating when I'm on a roll and want to get something finished, but I've learned the hard way to pace myself and not push too hard.

Another way I manage my fatigue is by having a dedicated sewing room. Again, I'm aware a lot of people won't have this luxury, but sewing is my life and my therapy, and we have thankfully been able to prioritise a space that I can use just for sewing. Having a dedicated sewing room means I don't have to tidy things away at the end, when my energy levels are at their lowest. I can just leave everything out. I have also arranged my sewing space so that everything is within arm's reach. It's all just there – I don't have to use excess energy moving from one area to another. For example, I have my ironing station right next to my sewing station. Pressing is a hugely important process in sewing, one that was drilled into me at school by my textiles teacher, so I sew and press, sew and press. Making sure my iron is within arm's reach of my sewing machine means I'm not moving around constantly, so I can preserve my energy levels.

Another thing I can find challenging is maintaining concentration and I often end up making mistakes – more than I get it right, usually! I easily forget things and in order to cope with this, I make sure that, in my sewing room, everything has its place. Everything is on hooks on pin boards. I try to be really strict with myself about putting things away in the right places when I've finished with them. My short-term memory is affected by my MS, so it helps when everything has a set place.

My hands are also affected by my condition, which can obviously cause me challenges with sewing. My hands are fine on some days; on others they aren't. My finger tips are always numb, which means I find hand sewing very difficult, not being able to grip the needle. I don't use straight pins for the same reasons. Instead, I use fabric clips, which are amazing and I wouldn't be without them. I also tend to prioritise projects that don't involve hand sewing.

I'm a wheelchair user and find I can't use a foot pedal on a sewing machine effectively. It's difficult to control the pressure and thus the speed of the

"My main piece of advice is to remember that it's just fabric. The world won't end if you get it wrong or make a mistake. Most mistakes can be rectified and we learn more from our mistakes than we do when we get things right."

machine. So, I use a sewing machine that has a stop-start button, which means I am able to control the action of the sewing machine with my hands, and this works brilliantly. My cover stitch and overlocker machines currently don't have stop-start buttons, so I counter this by positioning the pedals against my body and use my body weight to control them. It's not a perfect system but, until sewing machines catch up, it works for me! In my opinion, all sewing machines should have an automatic needle-threader and a stop-start button. Threading a machine without a needle threader is very difficult for me as I don't have the motor control over my hands. I currently have a manual threading overlocker and it can take me all day to thread it up if I need to! I tend to ask my husband to thread it up for me, which can be very frustrating if it unthreads and he isn't on hand. One day I'll have an air threader overlocker, which would be much easier, but this is how I make it work until that day comes.

Using a wheelchair in my sewing room can also be tricky, as it's a large chair with a bag on the back and my sewing space isn't very big. I deal with this by transferring to a wheelie office chair when I'm sewing. It means I'm able to wheel between my sewing machines much more easily.

WHAT CHALLENGES DO YOU FACE WITH CLOTHING?

Some of my issues with clothing are because of being a wheelchair user, and some are because I'm menopausal, meaning I experience a lot of bloating around my stomach. Clothing must be comfortable when I'm sitting down. The body changes when you're seated: you spread out and your crotch and hip measurements change dramatically. I cannot tolerate wearing anything tight around my tummy. I also find it very uncomfortable to have lots of fabric under my bottom and legs, and big flowy skirts just get caught in the wheels. These factors really inform my choice of clothing and the sewing patterns I choose to make. Something else I'm aware of is that, when you're sitting in a wheelchair, suddenly your bust is very much on show. This causes me to be selective with my necklines as I'm conscious everyone is above me looking down.

To work for a seated figure, trousers, for example, need to be higher in the back and lower in the front, and the legs need to be longer as they ride up when you sit. I also need more room around the top of the legs, and the waist and crotch because of the way my body changes when I'm sitting in my chair. I'm able to make these adjustments to the garments I make for myself, but clothes in shops don't ever accommodate this sort of thing.

Something I do as a wheelchair user is wear an item on my top half that has some interesting feature. I want to draw people's attention away from the chair so, if I'm wearing something with a statement sleeve or some kind of decoration around the neckline, it means their focus is on the top half of me.

I know my own measurements and adjustments very well now, after years of practice at adapting the sewing patterns I use. This makes it a lot easier for me to make my own clothes, knowing they will fit perfectly.

ANY TIPS OR ADVICE?

My main piece of advice is to remember that it's just fabric. The world won't end if you get it wrong or make a mistake. Most mistakes can be rectified and we learn more from our mistakes than we do when we get things right. If you get stuck in your head and don't start for fear of getting it wrong, you'll stop yourself from getting going. No matter what you do, it won't be a total disaster. I have a project, a beautiful Chanel-style jacket, which I would love to make. However, it involves a lot of hand sewing, and the fear of not being able to manage it means the project has sat in my sewing room for a really long time. I will make it; I just don't know when. I do know I simply need to push past my fear of failing at it and make a start – as I said, it's just fabric.

I tissue fit everything I make first. Making a toile uses a lot of energy and also involves the cost of the extra fabric. I cut the pattern from Swedish tissue paper so that I can adjust and fit the garment before I have even started with fabric. It's a much easier process, as you can sew the tissue paper, and making adjustments is simpler, meaning I have a lot more energy in my reserves to sew the actual garment. I then keep my tissue patterns so I can use them again in future projects. Even without having to make accommodations in my sewing practice to allow for my disability, I would still use Swedish tissue paper to test my pattern's fit, as it makes the whole process so straightforward!

As I've mentioned before, how you set up your workspace is very important in making sewing accessible, and I've explained how I've made things work for me. With your sewing room, make sure you have the right support so that you are comfortable, the right lighting and the right temperature control for you. The environment you work in is very important. As far as possible, you need to design it to help yourself function effectively and not make your health worse.

Because of the memory problems that are part of my condition, it helps me to get my head around something if I talk through a project or process out loud before I begin. I've also learned that, if you want to remember something, singing it can help, as singing causes information to be stored in a different part of the brain. I will often talk through the steps of a project with my husband. I'm not expecting him to understand or to have any input, but just to act as a listening ear while I say it out loud. This helps my brain process what I need to do.

Over time, I've learned what does and doesn't work for me. I don't bother to put pockets in and I don't add lumpy decorative details such as rivets, which would be uncomfortable to sit on. I choose to use fastenings that work with my needs. If a pattern calls for a fly zip to be inserted, for example, I don't bother

to put one in because I have no use for it and it can be uncomfortable. When you make, or adapt, your own clothes, you have the freedom to change a pattern to work for you. You write the rules.

An item I wouldn't be without in my sewing kit is my pair of spring-loaded scissors, as these help reduce hand fatigue. I also tend to find it easier to use the thread cutter on my machine rather than a pair of snips. Alongside my scissors, I have a rotary cutter in my kit, which is vital. My husband, who does the majority of my cutting-out, has arthritis and he finds a rotary cutter much easier to use.

Yvonne's Top Tips

1. Don't be afraid to ask for help if it means you can protect your energy levels for other things.

2. Have everything within arm's reach so that you aren't expending unnecessary energy reaching for things.

3. Have a clear place for everything and be strict about putting things back correctly so you always know where they are.

4. Tissue fit your projects first to check the fit without exerting yourself sewing up a toile.

5. Talk through the steps out loud to someone else to help your brain process what you need to do in each stage.

I mentioned before that I wouldn't be without my fabric clips. I can't use straight pins and originally was using bulldog clips to hold my fabric in place – until I discovered fabric clips. Now I use them all the time.

I love all different types of fabric, but my favourite to sew with and wear is jersey. It's so comfortable because it has a natural stretch. I always choose a natural fibre jersey, such as cotton, as this is very important when you are in a wheelchair. I can perspire a lot in my chair and natural fibres help to draw moisture away from the body. Jersey also doesn't crease much; another important thing I look for in a fabric.

I also love viscose challis and cotton sateen. I've been using these fabrics a lot in my most recent makes and they are beautiful to work with and lovely to wear. They're breathable too. They feel very feminine and light and make lovely dresses.

Fabrics I would definitely avoid are anything that needs a lot of ironing, or creases easily. Also, fabrics that can become uncomfortable when you wear them for prolonged periods of time, such as non-stretch denim. A fabric must be able to help me regulate my temperature too, keeping me cool in the heat, and warm in the winter; it must be made from natural fibres, and be able to move with me so that I can look stylish and stay comfortable in my chair.

Meet the Maker
Favourite Tools

1. SWEDISH TISSUE PAPER
2. FABRIC CLIPS
3. SPRING-LOADED SCISSORS

Yvonne Coleclough

You can find Yvonne on FB & IG
@thewheeliestitcher

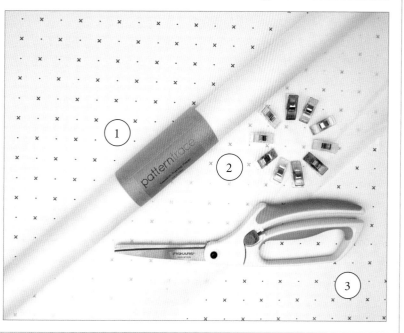

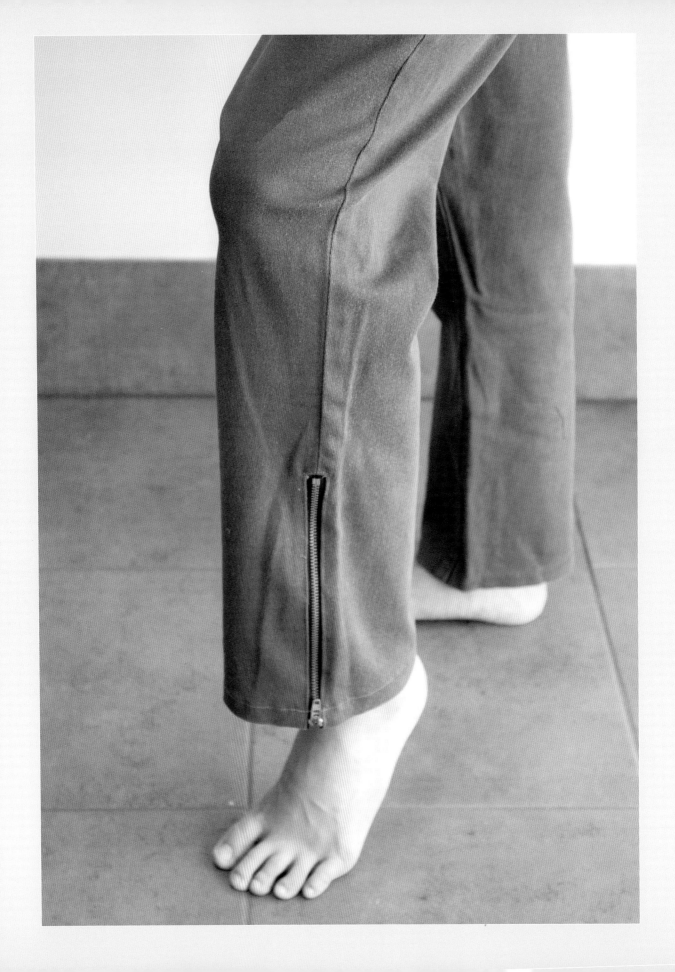

PROJECT 1

INSERTING ZIPS INTO TROUSER HEMS

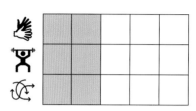

Trousers can be difficult to put on at the best of times. They can be even harder to put on if you have access or dexterity challenges. This project involves inserting zips into the hem side seams of your trousers, meaning the bottoms can be opened for easier dressing. This is great for prosthesis wearers, those who may experience ankle swelling, mobility issues or fatigue issues. It also means trousers can be put on over shoes, avoiding the necessity for shoes to be removed for dressing. This project can also mean easy access to the lower legs for medical treatment. In addition to this, it makes for a really stylish upcycle detail to an old pair of trousers. You choose the length of the zip and how many seams you put zips into. Full access your way!

What you will need:

- A pair of trousers
- 1, 2, 3 or 4 metal coil zips depending on how many seams you wish to use.
- Straight pins or fabric basting glue
- Fabric pen or chalk pencil
- Ruler
- Stitch ripper or snips
- Fabric scissors
- Vlieseline Bondaweb T10 Tape
- Iron and ironing board, or similar
- Zipper foot
- Sewing machine
- Matching sewing thread

If you have dexterity challenges and find zips difficult to fasten, try inserting a zip with a ring pull for ease.

1. Identify which seams you want to insert your zips into.

2. Position your zip alongside the seam and, using a straight pin or fabric marker, mark the length of the opening required to be able to insert the zip. Remember that you won't be able to stitch through the metal coil.

3. Use a ruler and fabric marker to draw a line on each side of the seam line, from your straight pin to the hem, 0.5cm (¼") away from the seam line. Join up these lines with a horizontal line across the top where your straight pin sits.

4. Now draw a triangle from the corners to the seam.

5. Using snips or a stitch ripper, open up the leg seam only as far as the point of the triangle.

6. Snip along the sides of the triangle to the corners (but not quite all the way).

7. Turn the trouser leg inside out and apply Vlieseline Bondaweb T10 Tape down both long sides of the opening, and across the short end, by placing the tape, glue side down, and heating with your iron.

8. Peel off the paper from the tape and fold the fabric back along your drawn lines. Use your iron to fix the fabric in place with the Bondaweb glue.

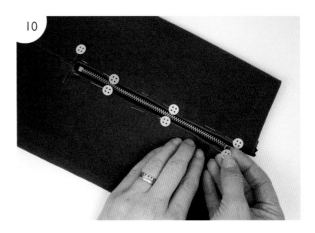

9. Turn the trouser leg back the right way round. Your opening should now be a neat rectangle running along the seam of the trousers.

10. Place the zip underneath this opening, with the zipper pull at the hem. The coil should sit neatly in the space you have created, with some of the tape visible all the way round. Pin or glue baste the zip in place.

11. Attach a zipper foot to your sewing machine. Edge stitch all the way round the opening, starting at one end of the hem, pivoting at the top corner, along the top, pivoting at the second corner, and back down the other side, finishing at the other end of the hem.

12. Check that the zipper pull slides up and down easily without getting caught.

13

13. Turn up the hem, enclosing the ends of the zipper tape, and top stitch in place. Repeat this process for any other seams you wish to open up.

Top Tips

» To make it easier to sew in your zipper, move the zipper pull out of the way as your zipper foot moves past it. Do this by leaving your needle in the fabric, lifting your zipper foot, then sliding the zipper pull up or down the coil to move it past the zipper foot. You can then lower the presser foot and continue your line of stitching uninterrupted.

» Often, a pair of trousers will be constructed using a run and fell seam on the inside leg and a straight seam on the outside leg. If this is the case for you, I recommend choosing the straight seam to work with, as this will make the alteration much easier to do.

» If you have dexterity challenges and find zips difficult to fasten, try inserting a zip with a ring pull for ease.

PROJECT 2

POPPER TAPE SLEEVE OPENING

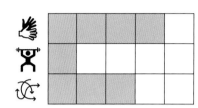

If you've ever wished you could gain access to parts of your body without needing to get undressed, this is the project for you. It's also a great alteration to make to your clothes if you find zips challenging, either to insert or to fasten. Here, you will learn how to create an opening in the sleeve of a top, which is great if you need access to your arms for any reason, for example, for medical treatment. However, this project can be transferred to any part of a garment, according to your access needs: the hems of trousers, cuffs on a jacket, the front of shirts – you name it, the process is the same.

Using a zipper foot on your sewing machine for sewing in the popper tape will make it much easier to navigate round the lumpy poppers.

What you will need:

- A long-sleeved garment
- Popper (or snap) tape
- Straight pins
- Safety pins (optional)
- Non-heat-erasable fabric pen or chalk pencil
- Ruler
- Interfacing
- Iron and ironing board, or similar
- Small embroidery scissors or snips
- Fabric glue (optional)
- Cotton tape 2.5cm (1") wide
- Sewing machine
- Zipper foot
- Matching sewing thread
- Contrast sewing thread
- Hand sewing needles
- Needle puller (optional)
- Needle threader (optional)

1.   Using a ruler and your chosen fabric marker (not heat erasable), draw a line down the centre of your sleeve where you want your opening to be.

2.   With the fabric marker, mark the end points of your opening. This can be as big as you need it to be.

3.   Place straight pins at the two end points you marked in step 2. This will mean that, when you turn your sleeve inside out in the next step, you will be able to easily see where these points are. You can also use safety pins for this step.

4.   Cut a piece of interfacing that is slightly longer than the distance between your two straight pins and approximately 3cm (1 ⅛") wide. Turn your sleeve inside out and apply the interfacing, using your iron, along the line you have marked. Make sure the two pins are also covered.

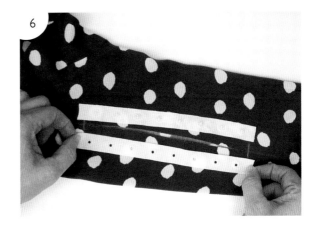

5. Turn the sleeve back to the right side and remove the marker pins. Using snips or small embroidery scissors, cut along the line you have drawn from one end point to the other. You should be cutting through the fabric and the interfacing.

6. Cut a length of popper tape 1–2cm (⅜"– ⅝") longer than the slit you have made.

7. Take the male side of the popper tape. Position it along one of the raw

edges of the opening, so that you are looking at the right side of both the tape and the sleeve, with the tape hanging over the lip of the raw edge. Taking a very small seam allowance from the sleeve, tack the edge of

the tape into place. This will help hold it while you stitch it on the sewing machine. Use a needle puller to help you pull the needle through more easily, if required.

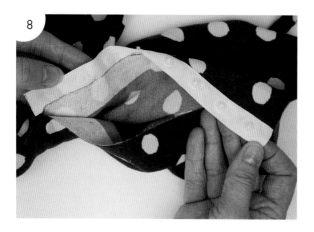

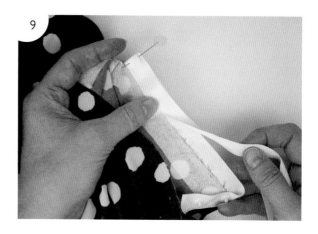

8. Using the sewing machine, top stitch the popper tape in place along this line of tacking. Remove the tacking thread.

9. Cut a length of cotton tape slightly longer than the popper tape. Turning the end under, pin the cotton tape over the underside of the popper tape, enclosing the raw seam you just stitched.

10. Tack the cotton tape in place all the way round its four sides.

11. Attach a zipper foot to your sewing machine. Edge stitch all the way round the four sides of the popper tape and cotton tape, following the tacking line. Remove the tacking threads and tuck the tapes inside the sleeve.

12. Attach the female side of the popper tape to the male side. Using

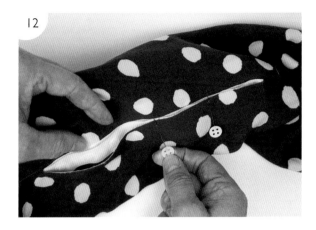

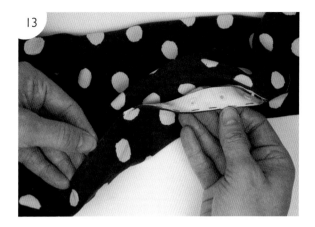

this as a marker for placement, pin (or clip, if preferred) the female tape to the other raw edge of the sleeve opening. This time the tape should be sitting inside the sleeve, wrong side to wrong side.

13. Without removing the pins, undo the popper tape. Leave the pins in position for as long as you can as they will stop the tape moving out of place, resulting in the poppers not lining up.

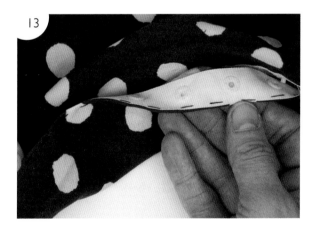

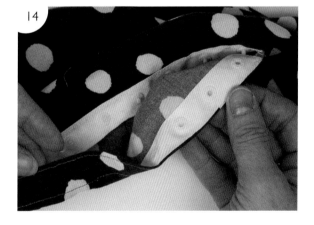

Turn under the other raw edge of the opening a very small amount and tack the tape in place along this edge.

14. Top stitch all the way round the popper tape using a zipper foot, securing it in place and enclosing the raw edge of the sleeve. Remove the tacking threads.

15. Close up the popper tape to check for alignment, and your sleeve opening is complete.

Top Tips

» Using a zipper foot on your sewing machine for sewing in the popper tape will make it much easier to navigate round the lumpy poppers.

» If you find hand sewing challenging, fabric basting glue, fabric clips or straight pins can be used as an alternative. However, a hand sewn tacking stitch will definitely make the machine sewing easier for this project, so maybe using a needle puller would help.

» Use thread in a contrasting colour for your tacking stitches to make them easy to see when removing them.

PROJECT 3

INSERTING A HORIZONTAL ZIP INTO A DRESS WAIST

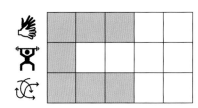

If you need access to your waist while wearing a dress, this can mean having to completely lift the skirt, which isn't very convenient when out in public. Should you need to access a stoma bag, nephrostomy bags, a feeding tube, or maybe a wound dressing following a C-section or key hole surgery, dresses are probably a tricky addition to your wardrobe. This project can change all that. By inserting a zip into the waist of your dress, you can easily access your body as needed. This can be done in the front or the back and, by using an invisible zip, can mean that the addition to your garment won't spoil the look of your dress.

For a more statement feature, you can use a chunky or contrasting colour zip in place of the discreet invisible zip.

What you will need:

- A dress
- An invisible zip slightly shorter than the measurement from side seam to side seam
- Stitch ripper or snips
- Fabric scissors
- Vlieseline T20 Edge Tape
- Iron and ironing board, or similar
- Fabric pen or chalk pencil
- Straight pins or fabric basting glue
- Invisible zipper foot (optional)
- Sewing machine
- Matching sewing thread

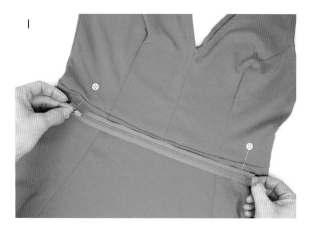

1.   To mark where the zip will go on your dress, lay the zip onto the garment and mark the start and end position with straight pins or a fabric marker. You want this measurement to be slightly shorter than the length of the zip.

2.   Using a stitch ripper or snips, open up the seam between the two points you marked in step 1. If your dress doesn't have a seam at the waist, see Top Tips.

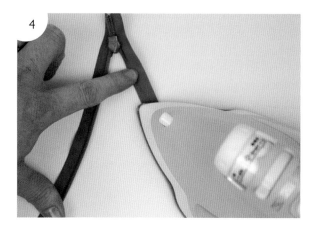

3.   Turn the dress inside out and apply Vlieseline T20 Edge Tape along the edges of the opening, using your iron. This will help prevent the fabric from stretching.

4.   Again using your iron, press open the coil on your invisible zip. This will make it easier to sew into your seam.

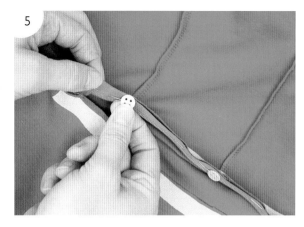

5. With the dress inside out, place the zip face down along the seam opening. Pin or glue one side of the zipper tape to the seam edge of the dress, right sides together. You can do this by turning the seam allowance back on itself and lining up the raw edge with the edge of the zipper tape.

6. Using an invisible zipper foot on your sewing machine, stitch along this side of the zipper tape, running the needle along the groove where the

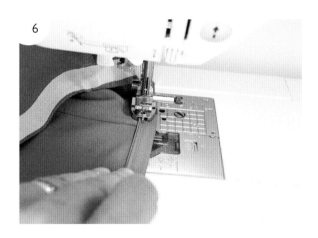

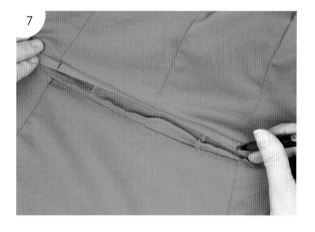

coil folds back on itself. By pressing the coil back, finding this groove becomes much easier. The closer you can stitch to the coil of the zip, the more invisible the zip will be.

7. Close up the zip to check the pull runs smoothly and you haven't caught the coil with your machine needle. At this point, I like to transfer any seam lines, or details I wish to have lined up when the zipper is closed, onto the other side of the zipper tape with a fabric marker. When the zip is then

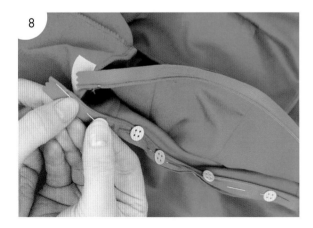

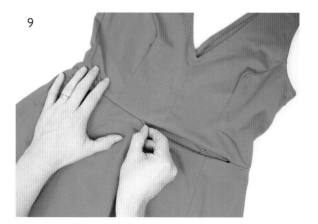

opened again, you can use these marks to line up the other side of the zip.

8. Repeat step 5 with the other side of the zipper tape and stitch in place.

9. Turn the dress back through to the right side. Tuck the zip inside the dress opening and pull the zipper closed to check it runs smoothly. Your waist opening is now complete.

Top Tips

» If your dress doesn't have a waist seam, you can create one to sew your zip into. Mark a horizontal line across the body where you wish the opening to be. Follow step 1, marking the two end points of the zip on this line, and use snips or scissors to cut along it to open the fabric.

» If you don't have access to an invisible zipper foot for your sewing machine, this step can also be done using an adjustable piping foot. In the absence of both of these, a regular zipper foot can be used. However, the best results will be achieved using a specialist presser foot.

» For a more statement feature, you can use a chunky or contrasting colour zip in place of the discreet invisible zip.

PROJECT 4

MAGNETIC BUTTONS

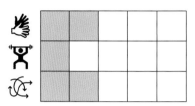

Buttons can be frustrating at the best of times. Add in dexterity or fatigue complications and they can be the worst of fastenings. There is even a clinical fear of buttons known as koumpounophobia, which affects a large number of people. Although, in this project, I have suggested stitching the buttons back onto the shirt, this part can be skipped. Using magnetic fastenings in place of buttons is a great way to make garments such as shirts more accessible.

Please note the use of magnets in clothing is not recommended if the wearer has a pacemaker. You should consult your medical practitioner if you have any queries about this.

What you will need:

- A button front shirt
- Magnetic buttons
- Small embroidery scissors or snips
- Stitch ripper
- Straight pins or fabric clips
- Fabric pen or chalk pencil
- Sewing machine
- Button applying foot (optional)
- Matching sewing thread
- Hand sewing needles (optional)
- Needle puller (optional)
- Needle threader (optional)

1. Pair up your magnetic buttons so you have one pair for each button on the shirt, making sure they attract each other.

2. Using snips or small embroidery scissors, cut off all the buttons you are replacing with magnets, and put them to one side. Remove any remaining threads.

3. On the buttonhole side of the shirt, use a stitch ripper or small embroidery scissors to unpick the line of stitching of the placket.

4. Separate the pairs of magnetic buttons and insert one from each pair underneath the buttonhole placket. Make sure you put the magnets in

the correct way up so they attract the other half. As you won't be able to remove the buttonholes from the shirt, the magnets need to be inserted as close to the buttonholes as possible. Push them into the fold on the edge of the placket and pin or clip them in place through the plastic surround. In

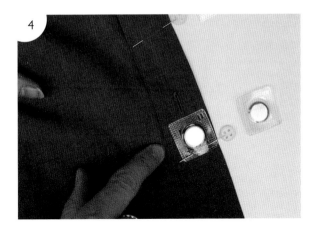

the image, the third magnet is shown on the outside of the placket to demonstrate the positioning. However, the magnets need to be inside the placket, as shown with the first two.

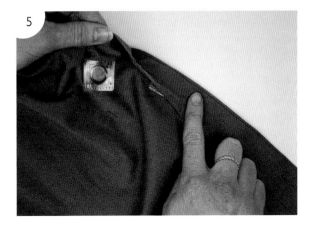

5. Sew a line of top stitching along the fold of the placket, catching in the edge of the plastic surrounds as you go. This will hold the magnets in place.

6. Next, sew a line of top stitching down the other side of the buttonhole placket, along the line you unpicked in step 3. The magnets are now fully enclosed inside the placket.

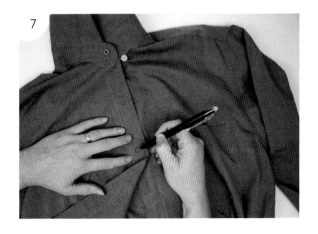

7. Place a straight pin or fabric clip at the top if the shirt placket, holding the shirt closed. Laying the button placket over the magnetised buttonhole placket, use a fabric marker to mark the positions of the inserted magnets, through the fabric, onto the button placket.

8. Unpick the line of stitching holding the button placket closed, as you did in step 3 on the buttonhole side.

9. Repeat the process you did in step 4, this time with the opposite magnets, lining up the magnets with the position marks you made in step 7. Pin them in place through the plastic casing.

10. Repeat steps 5 and 6 on the button placket side, securing and encasing the magnets within it.

11. Attach a button applying foot to your sewing machine. Position the buttons over the top of the buttonholes and stitch them in place. You can do this by hand if you don't have a button applying foot for your sewing

machine, or if you prefer to hand sew. When finished, it should give the illusion of the buttons being fastened with the buttonholes when the shirt front is closed.

12. Close up the front of your shirt by laying the placket with the buttonholes and buttons over the top of the other placket to check the positioning. Your magnetic-fastening shirt is now complete.

Top Tips

» The magnets will try to stick to the plate of your sewing machine as you sew them, so you will need to take charge of them and guide them through the machine as you sew.

» Be careful when you iron your shirt as the plastic surrounds on the magnets will melt. Try to avoid ironing over the plackets once you have inserted your magnets.

» If you need a stronger fastening, use additional magnets in the plackets for greater magnetisation.

PROJECT 5

INSERTING A BUTTONHOLE IN A POCKET

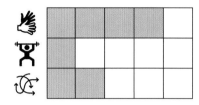

This project is perfect if you have a PEG feeding tube or an insulin pump. By making this simple alteration to your garments with pockets, you can have easy access to your tubes without needing to undress.

When deciding where to position your buttonhole, remember, the lower down it is on the pocket bag, the harder it will be to access when you are wearing your trousers. The higher up it is, the more difficult it will be to sew, and there is more chance of the buttonhole showing when you are wearing the garment. However, it will be easier to access when the trousers are worn. Bear this in mind when choosing where to sew your buttonhole.

What you will need:

- A pair of trousers with pockets
- A buttonhole foot
- Sewing machine
- Matching sewing thread
- Stitch ripper or snips
- A small square of interfacing
- Iron and ironing board, or similar
- Fabric pen or chalk pencil
- Straight pins

PROJECT 5 – Inserting a buttonhole in a pocket

1. Decide which pocket you wish to insert the buttonhole opening into. Bear in mind any rivets or metal trims on your garment, as these will make the alteration harder to do.

2. Using a stitch ripper, or snips, open up the bottom of the pocket bag.

3. Cut a small square of interfacing (big enough to accommodate your buttonhole). Position it on the outside of your pocket bag, in the general area where you'd like to stitch your buttonhole, and fix it in place with your iron.

4. Place a straight pin in the interfaced fabric on the outside of the pocket bag (through one layer of fabric only or you will end up sewing your pocket bag shut!) where you want the buttonhole to sit.

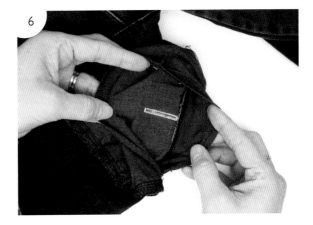

5. On the inside of the pocket bag, you will be able to see the pin. Mark this place with a fabric marker. You can now remove the pin.

6. Use your mark as a guide as to where to stitch your buttonhole and, using a buttonhole foot (or whatever settings you have on your sewing machine), stitch the buttonhole in place. Stitch the longest buttonhole your sewing machine will allow, for easier access.

Top Tips

» When deciding where to position your buttonhole, remember, the lower down it is on the pocket bag, the harder it will be to access when you are wearing your trousers. The higher up it is, the more difficult it will be to sew, and there is more chance of the buttonhole showing when you are wearing the garment. However, it will be easier to access when the trousers are worn. Bear this in mind when choosing where to sew your buttonhole.

» When opening your buttonhole, work from one end into the centre, and then the other end into the centre. This will help prevent slipping and slicing through the bar tack stitching at the ends of your buttonhole.

» Make sure you are completely satisfied with the positioning of your buttonhole before opening it up. Once it is cut, it can't be moved!

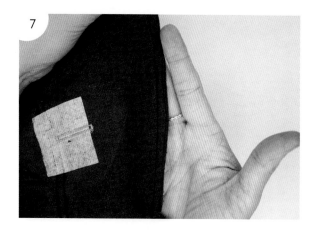

7. Stitch up the bottom of the pocket bag again to close the opening you made.

8. Open up the buttonhole, using a stitch ripper or embroidery scissors, by cutting down the centre line inside the stitching.

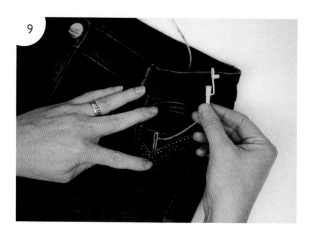

9. Pass your tube end through the buttonhole and tuck it inside your pocket.

Alycia Hirani

Alycia was born with osteogenesis imperfecta, otherwise known as brittle bones disease. She has turned her love of crafting and sewing as a child into a business, making beautiful bespoke garments.

> *"If you want to get into sewing, start with something small. Inch towards what you want to make. It doesn't have to be perfect — only you will know if you've made any mistakes! Anything that goes wrong just makes for learning for the next project!"*

HOW DID YOU GET INTO SEWING?

I was born with my condition but for as long as I can remember I have loved crafting. My bones are weak, can break easily, and I experience a lot of fatigue so, as a child, I wasn't able to go out to play in the playground with the other children. I would entertain myself with drawing and crafting initially, sitting at my table in the classroom, and this is where my love for creating began. Nothing held me back while I sat at my desk with everything within arm's reach, so it became a huge outlet for me. However, even back then, my love for the creative arts was met with resistance from teachers and staff, as the focus at school was always on the importance of the academic subjects; art was passed off as unimportant, but it was important to me.

In high school, I was introduced to sewing through home economics/textiles lessons, and something just clicked for me. I loved it. It was an activity I could do while sitting down so it was accessible for me, and there was something about being able to turn a two-dimensional pattern into a three-dimensional garment that would fit a body that really appealed to me.

So I was hooked. I found it fascinating. I've also always loved maths, and the analytical side of pattern cutting and sewing appealed to both these sides of me. It felt as though the body was being treated like architecture and I knew this was what I wanted to do. At university, I studied fashion design with design for performance and, while there, I discovered corsetry. What I love about corsetry is it's a garment that can adapt to support and shape the body. My aim with any corset is to make the wearer feel supported, and look and feel beautiful. It's not about the garment for me – it's about making the person feel special.

WHAT CHALLENGES HAVE YOU FOUND WITH ACCESSING THE CRAFT?

My main challenge was accessing professional work in the industry. I decided early on that I wanted to work for myself so that I could work around and accommodate my own disability. A lot of my tutors at university cautioned me that this would be hard, but I just didn't feel there was a place for me in the industry at the time. The fashion and costume industries are so fast paced and I knew I'd never be able to keep up. I didn't feel as though the industry was ready to include me. I'm not even sure it would be today. Things are much better than they were, but I find it's only very specialised projects that can understand and accommodate the different needs I have. Even now, I feel apprehensive about going into projects for fear of not being accommodated effectively, though I've come a long way. I would always rather approach with caution and course-correct than overpromise what I'm able to manage.

Travel can be difficult; any moving and heavy lifting is often out of my remit. With brittle bones, your body can develop differently. As such, I am of short stature, so I can't offer to reach things on high shelves or use high drafting tables. As I said before, the pace of the fashion and costume industries is so great that, even if they wanted to put accommodations in place, there often just doesn't seem to be the time.

I know myself and my condition very well. I'm a slow, methodical sewer and this also doesn't go with certain work scenarios. Bridal shops, for example, need things sewn within a certain time frame. Time is money, as it is in any industry, and I personally prefer to take my time and put care into the things I create; that's more important to me than speed and quantity. I couldn't do a fast-paced job anyway as I'd wear myself out! So, from an early point in my adult life, I realised I'd have to do it myself rather than search externally for work that suited what I wanted to do, and which could accommodate my disability and needs.

Emiah, my business, started as an outlet when I was at university – a very expensive hobby, but a way to decompress from the stress of higher education. Once university was over, however, I found myself a little lost now that I didn't have the structure of education to fall back on. I didn't know what to do with myself or what to do next. I now needed to do everything myself and that felt incredibly overwhelming, so I just drifted for a while. I continued sewing because that's what I've always done, and I was able to work at my own pace, honouring my own abilities, energy levels, and desires, making things I loved. I am a huge perfectionist and finding balance is always a struggle. I regularly burn myself out by pushing just that little too far, so it was nice not to have people relying on me for things.

I've now learned to put additional safeguards in place to help me manage my body and energy levels. For example, I have an alarm set on my phone every hour, reminding me to stretch, as I tend to lose track of time when I'm sitting at the sewing machine. I've also adapted my sewing space and kit in the way that's best for me, so it's easier to work in that area.

WHAT CHALLENGES DO YOU FACE WITH CLOTHING?

Clothing has always been a challenge for me. High street clothing isn't designed to fit most people in the real world; it's designed to fit some arbitrary figure that doesn't actually exist. I do like to get out and see and feel clothes in the real world, but this is getting harder with the disappearance of the high street and the prevalence of online shopping.

For me personally, because of my short stature, clothes are always too long. I learned how to turn up a hem very early on in my sewing journey. I've also learned how off-the-peg clothing can serve me – for example, I now know that a skirt sold as a midi length is actually a maxi skirt for me. And I've learned to adapt both my physical clothing and what I look for when I'm shopping. An example of this would be that garments with a defined waistline don't always sit in the right place on my shorter torso, so I tend to opt for more cropped or empire line styles, which then work for me.

I'm a manual wheelchair user and I use crutches, so I need my garments to work for both sitting and standing. When I'm hemming something to fit me, I will always ask someone to pin the hem for me. I have scoliosis of the spine, so my skirt lengths are hardly ever level all the way around. To take account of this, we pin the entire hem in several places and take our time to make sure this part is right. I've worked out that if I have the hem of my skirts pinned so they touch the floor, this is a good visual to check

> "I keep my sewing space as linear as possible. This helps me avoid needing to move around too much."

they are level on me. I then cut the hem at this length and by the time I've turned it up, it's the correct length so I'm not going to step on or trip over it.

In Indian culture, making your own clothes, or having them made for you, is common practice. Indian clothes aren't traditionally made for my body shape so I've always adapted my own. This gives me more control over what I get to wear. Indian tops or blouses, which we wear with saris or long skirts, can be traditionally quite cropped and, as I prefer to cover my midriff, I have always requested a longer blouse. When these were made for me, they would sometimes add pleats, which made me feel and look really frumpy. Now I do them myself and just make them slightly longer in the body and tailored to my measurements.

Another adaptation I often make to my Indian clothes is to the fastening at the back. Traditionally, they are fastened with hooks and eyes or zips, which are helpful but can be awkward to adjust and fasten. I prefer to make a pseudo-corset back to mine using some light boning and fabric loops, and fastening with some ribbon or lacing. This means I can easily adjust the fit if I fluctuate in size, without having to keep amending the seams, while at the same time making it a design feature.

If I'm going to be using my wheelchair, I prefer to wear stretchy trousers. I find sitting in tight trousers so uncomfortable.

I will add elastic to everything for this reason too. Elasticated waistbands are far more comfortable than fixed ones. If I wear long, flowing skirts, I have to tuck them in so they don't get caught in the wheels. Alternatively, with shorter skirts, I'm conscious that one mistimed gust of wind could leave me more exposed than I care to be. To avoid this, I often wear lightweight shorts under a shorter skirt. I find this makes me feel more comfortable as well as protected. Additionally, something I look for in clothing and add to my own-made garments is wide armholes. I have limited range of movement when lifting my arms above my head due to my collarbones, so wider armholes make it much easier for me to get into a garment.

ANY TIPS OR ADVICE?

My main sewing room hack is using a mechanical table as my sewing table. I can adjust the height for seated or standing and this makes a huge difference to me. I also use a wheeled office chair so that I can move around easily and don't have to get up every time I want to get something. I have my sewing room set so that my desk is in front of me, and behind me I have a cube storage system that contains most of my tools and equipment. This means I can access everything I need by simply turning in my chair. I make sure to keep all my walkways clear and also have a cable management system set up under my desk. Avoiding trip hazards is very important for me in making my workspace accessible. Along with the cable management system, I have screwed a multi-point extension lead under my desk so that the sockets are higher up. This means I don't have to bend down to access the plugs.

I keep my sewing space as linear as possible. This helps me avoid needing to move around too much. I have a lot of trolleys on wheels as this means I can just wheel my equipment and projects around if I need to. I also have a footrest next to the foot pedal of my sewing machine. I find this helps avoid fatigue as, when I'm not using the foot pedal, I'm able to rest my foot comfortably.

My main advice when it comes to choosing a sewing machine is to pick one with a knee lift and a speed limiter. I have both these functions on my sewing machine and I find them so helpful. The knee lift frees up my hands to hold the part of my sewing project that needs supporting, while the speed limiter helps me avoid going too fast. I like to take things slow and steady and being able

"My main advice overall is to break down what you want to make into small steps and just take it one step at a time."

to control the maximum speed of my machine is a real plus point.

The main tool I use is a rotary cutter with a cutting mat. I find this much easier to use than scissors and will always cut with my rotary cutter if I can. Shears can be too heavy for my hands, and they can be really challenging on my grip strength, something I don't have a lot of. I prefer to use a symmetrical rotary cutter and hold it upright as this is much easier on my joints. Holding a rotary cutter in the traditional way can be a challenge for me due to my height and collar bones.

I have a couple of rotary cutters, one with a straight blade and one with a pinking blade. One thing I've never been able to use is pinking shears. They are often too heavy and awkward. A pinking blade on a rotary cutter works much better for me when the need arises.

One pair of scissors I do use often are a pair of duckbill scissors. I use a lot of French seams in my sewing, so these come in handy as I'm able to trim down seams without fear of catching the underneath of the seam allowance. Duckbill scissors are great as an accessible addition to your sewing kit because they mean it takes less effort and concentration to trim down seam allowances for all sewing projects.

I always have a pair of rubber-ended pliers in my kit too, as this helps with pulling straight pins and needles through fabric when I don't have the strength in my hands. Another item I wouldn't be without (and I own several) is an adjustable thimble. I could never get a thimble to work as I didn't really know how to use one and, as I like to wear my nails long, couldn't get them to fit my fingers. I also have hypermobility in my joints, so my fingertips have a lot of movement in them. I just don't like the feeling of them being enclosed in a traditional thimble. However, when I discovered adjustable thimbles, it changed everything for me. They sit on the front of the finger so can be worn with long nails and, because they are adjustable, I can make them fit me, even if my fingers swell.

When I'm cutting fabric pieces, I tend to use pattern weights instead of straight pins. I find it very difficult to push straight pins through lots of layers of fabric, or through an especially thick fabric, so using pattern weights avoids this necessity. I prefer to lay my larger fabric pieces out on the floor to cut them out. I lay several large cutting mats on the floor and have a pair of knee pads to make the process more comfortable. I do find this a lot of hard work, however, and will frequently find myself out of action for a couple of days after an extended cutting session. To help avoid this, I often ask someone to assist me with this part as it prevents complications in the long run.

When it comes to fabrics, I love a bit of luxury and sparkle. I do enjoy fabrics like chiffon but, as these are slippery,

Alycia's Top Tips

1. Set timers on your phone to remind yourself to move/stretch/drink water, to help support your body when you're in the sewing "zone".

2. Place your sewing machine on a mechanical table so that you can adjust the height for both standing and sitting.

3. Be sure to keep your walkways clear and move your sockets higher up to make your space safe to move around in and easily accessible.

4. Have all your equipment within arm's reach. A wheeled trolley means you don't have to carry everything around.

5. Choose a machine that has a speed limiter function so you can easily control the speed of your sewing machine.

they can be tricky to cut out and work with. One of my favourite fabrics to use is tulle as it adds volume and texture to a garment without fraying. It's a very forgiving fabric and quite easy to work with. I love to use lace also. You can use as little or as much as you want to add features to a garment. Any sorts of embellishment like this mean you can signpost where you want the eye to be drawn to. I'm a huge fabric magpie; I love to make something simple and elegant, then add a touch of sparkle to really lift it. Embellishments can be used to hide holes and stains, and a whole multitude of stitching sins.

I really like to wear stretch fabrics as I find them so comfortable, but I don't enjoy working with them. I feel as though stretch fabrics have a whole language of their own and it's not one I particularly want to learn. Instead, I add elastic to everything, and this gives me the movement and comfort I need.

My main advice overall is to break down what you want to make into small steps and just take it one step at a time. Practise your machine stitching, or your hand sewing, as this will help improve your skills; and there are so many resources and tips online if you want to learn something specific. I would also suggest, when you're first starting out, using a longer stitch length initially, to build your confidence. This will enable you to see quickly if something is working – and if it goes wrong, it's a lot faster to unpick!

Meet the Maker

Favourite Tools

Alycia Hirani

You can find Alycia on FB & IG @emiahcouture
www.emiah.co.uk

1. **ADJUSTABLE THIMBLE**

2. **DUCKBILL SCISSORS**

3. **SYMMETRICAL ROTARY CUTTER**

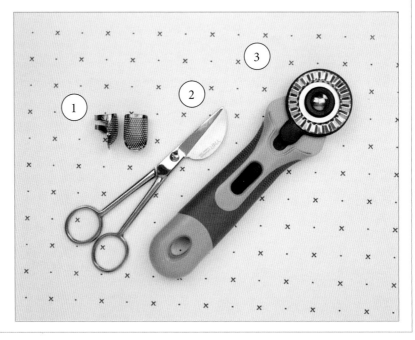

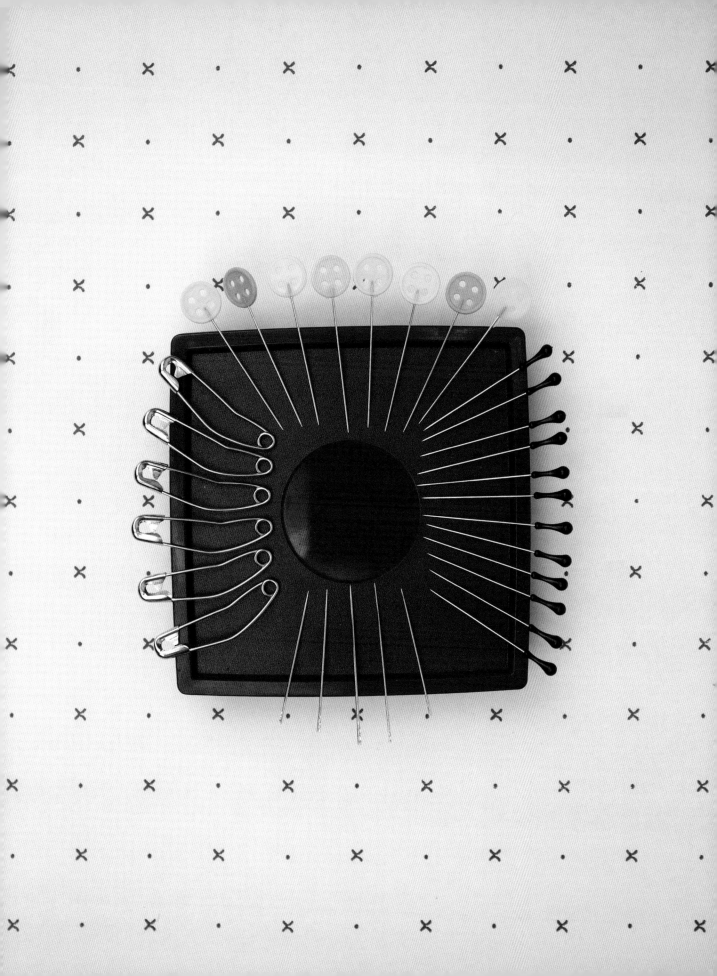

PROJECT 6

SHORTENING SLEEVES

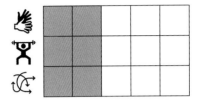

Knowing how to adjust the length of sleeves is a great addition to your sewing knowledge bank, as it has so many applications throughout life. Ill-fitting sleeves are fairly common with mass-produced clothing. If someone has arms of differing lengths, a limb difference or amputation, this project becomes even more important. It's also great for anyone with sensory issues around wearing long sleeves, or even just turning a cold-weather garment into a warm-weather one. This is one of the most versatile and important projects in this book.

This project focuses on altering the sleeves of a jersey garment. If you want to alter sleeves on a non-stretch garment, my advice is always to try to replicate how the original sleeve hem or cuff was constructed.

What you will need:

- A jersey top with long sleeves
- Tape measure
- Fabric pen or fabric chalk
- Fabric shears or rotary cutter and cutting mat
- Straight pins or fabric clips
- Overlocker (optional)
- Matching sewing thread

1. With your tape measure, from the shoulder, measure the length you wish the sleeve to be once altered. Remember to include the cuff in the measurement.

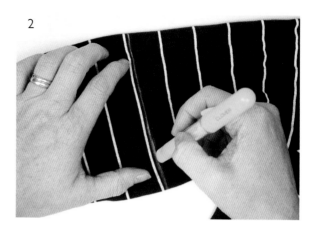

2. Mark the length using your fabric marker of choice.

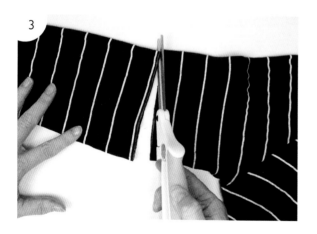

3. Cut the sleeve off at this point using fabric shears or a rotary cutter.

4. Separate the cuff from the sleeve by cutting off the overlocked edge, using your fabric shears or rotary cutter.

5

5. You will notice the cuff is smaller than the sleeve edge. This is exactly how it should be. In the next few steps, you will stretch the cuff to fit.

6

6. Using straight pins, or a fabric marker of your choice, mark the quarter points on the sleeve edge and on the cuff.

7

7. Slide the cuff onto the sleeve, right sides together, so that the raw edges of both are lined up. Match the quarter point markings and clip the cuff to the sleeve at these points.

8

8. When you sew the cuff to the sleeve end, you will need to stretch the fabric so that the cuff expands to fit the sleeve.

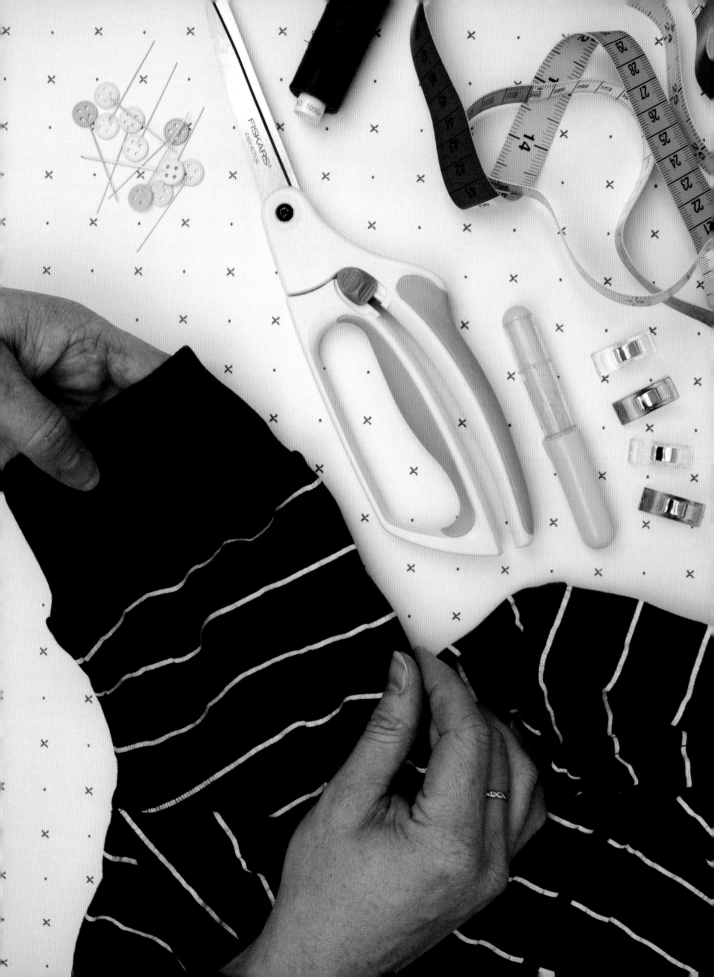

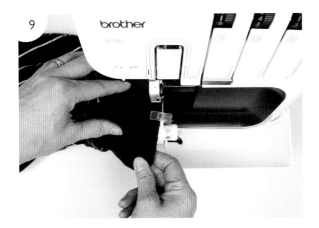

9. Stitch the cuff to the sleeve with your overlocker or alternative (see Top Tips), stretching the cuff to fit the sleeve as you go.

10. Pull the cuff down and your new sleeve is complete. Repeat on the second sleeve if required.

Top Tips

» This project focuses on altering the sleeves of a jersey garment. If you want to alter sleeves on a non-stretch garment, my advice is always to try to replicate how the original sleeve hem or cuff was constructed.

» Using fabric clips to fasten the cuff to the sleeve ready for stitching on the overlocker can help avoid slipping and hitting a pin with the blade of your overlocker.

» If you don't have an overlocker, using an overcasting stitch or stretch stitch on your sewing machine will allow the fabric to stretch.

PROJECT 7

SHORTENING / LENGTHENING JEANS

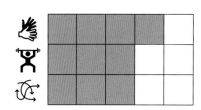

Similarly to being able to adjust sleeve lengths, knowing how to adjust the length of trousers is another staple in the world of sewing. It's an alteration I find myself doing time and time again. Should you be of short stature, or below average height, this is a project that is absolutely vital if you're shopping on the high street. Similarly, if you're taller than average height, finding trousers long enough can be a challenge. The additional difficulty here is that it's always easier to make things smaller than it is to make them bigger or longer. Not only is this relevant if you are tall, it's also relevant if you are a wheelchair user, as trousers need to be longer to accommodate a seated position. In this project, I show you how to make trousers both longer and shorter.

Try to avoid unpicking run and fell seams, for ease. Straight seams are much easier to reconstruct.

What you will need:

- A pair of jeans
- A second pair of jeans
- Tape measure
- Ruler
- Fabric pen or fabric chalk
- Pinking shears or pinking blade
- Fabric shears or rotary cutter and cutting mat
- Stitch ripper
- Fabric clips
- Sewing machine
- Matching sewing thread
- Iron and ironing board, or similar

Shortening jeans:

1.   Calculate how much you need to reduce the length of your trousers by. Turn the trouser leg inside out and measure where the new trouser hem needs to be. Mark this point with your fabric marker. In this example, I am reducing the length of the trousers by 13.5cm (5½").

2.   Move the tape measure down so the end sits inside the turned-up hem of the trousers. Make a note of the length

from the hem to the point marked in step 1. In this example, it is 12cm (4 ¾").

3.   Turn the trouser leg the right way out again. Fold the hem of the trousers up to the outside (ie the opposite way it would be turned up in a traditional hemming technique), so the distance from the hem turn-up to the new fold point is half the amount calculated in step 2. In this example, the measurement is 6cm (2 ⅜"). Clip the hem fold to hold it.

4.   Stitch along the groove of the top of the hem around the whole leg.

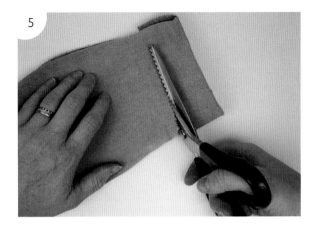

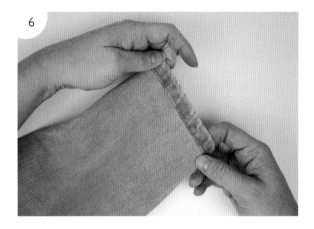

5. Turn the trouser leg inside out and cut away the excess fabric below your line of stitching, using pinking shears or a pinking blade on your rotary cutter.

6. Now turn the trouser leg the right way out again and tuck the hem fabric up inside the leg. You will have a shortened trouser leg featuring the hem's original decorative stitching. Repeat with the second leg, if necessary.

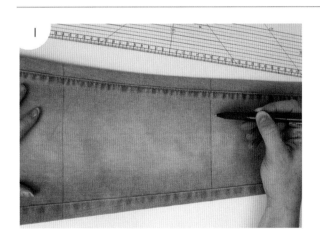

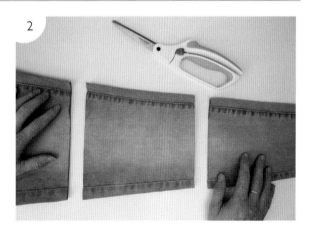

Lengthening jeans:

1. Calculate how much length you wish to add to your trousers. Divide this by two. Using your fabric marker, draw two lines, one at each position on the leg where you would like to add the extra fabric.

2. With your fabric shears or rotary cutter, cut the leg of the trousers along these lines.

3. Taking a stitch ripper, or tool of your choice, unpick the outside seam of the middle section. Then unpick approximately 7.5cm (3") of the side seam of the top and bottom sections. Make sure you unpick the same seam on all three sections.

4. From a second pair of jeans, cut two sections from the same side leg as the one you are working on. Make sure these two sections are enough to give you the finished length you require (see step 5).

5. Bear in mind, when working out how much fabric to add in, that you will need to include seam allowance on each horizontal seam. Where you have cut your original pair of trousers, you will lose a 1cm (⅜") seam allowance on each of these four edges (ie four x 1cm (⅜") overall). Make sure you add on this 4cm (1½") to your additional pieces. Likewise, you will lose a 1 cm (⅜") seam allowance from the edges of each part you are inserting. This also needs to be added in when cutting the additional panels.

For example, if I am increasing the length of my trouser legs by 20cm (8"), I will lose 4cm (1½") of seam allowance by reconstructing my chopped-up trousers. This means I need to cut 24cm (9½") worth of denim pieces from my second pair of trousers for each leg. If I decide to insert two pieces rather than one, say one at 15cm (6") and the second at 9cm (3½"), I will need to add seam allowance to each piece. This would make the pieces I need to cut 17cm (6 ¾") and 11cm (4¼"). Once all sewn together, this will leave the trouser legs at the required 20cm (8") longer in length. [No Pic]

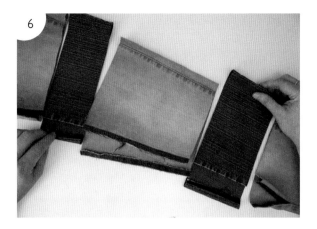

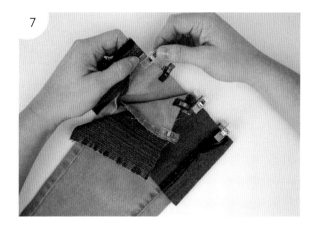

6. Unpick the outside side seam on each of these additional pieces.

7. Taking the bottom piece of the trouser leg and one of the additional panels, with right sides together, line up the side seams and clip or pin the

pieces together along the raw edges. Your added panel may be wider than your trouser legs, but that's ok. We will adjust this in a later step. However, it's important that the added panels aren't narrower than the original trouser leg.

8. Stitch along this edge with a 1cm (⅜") seam allowance. Open up the leg and press the seam.

9. Repeat step 8 with all the other trouser pieces until you have a complete trouser leg again. [No pic]

10. Turn the trouser leg inside out and trim any excess from the panels you have inserted, making sure they line up with the side seams of the trouser leg.

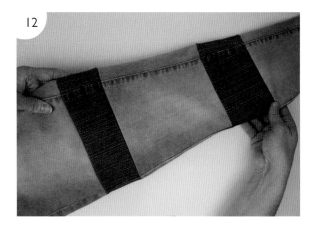

11. Line up the panel seams so that when you stitch up the side seams, the seam lines all match. Clip or pin in place to make sure they don't move out of position.

12. Stitch up the side seams, turn the trouser leg through to the right side, and press. Repeat with the other trouser leg, if required.

Top Tips

»   If you find the turned-up fabric on your shortened trousers pops out at the bottom of the hem, run some stitches along the side seams to catch down the excess fabric and hold it in place.

»   Try to avoid unpicking run and fell seams, for ease. Straight seams are much easier to reconstruct.

»   Make sure your second pair of jeans is as wide in the leg, or wider, than the pair you are adapting, to ensure you have enough fabric.

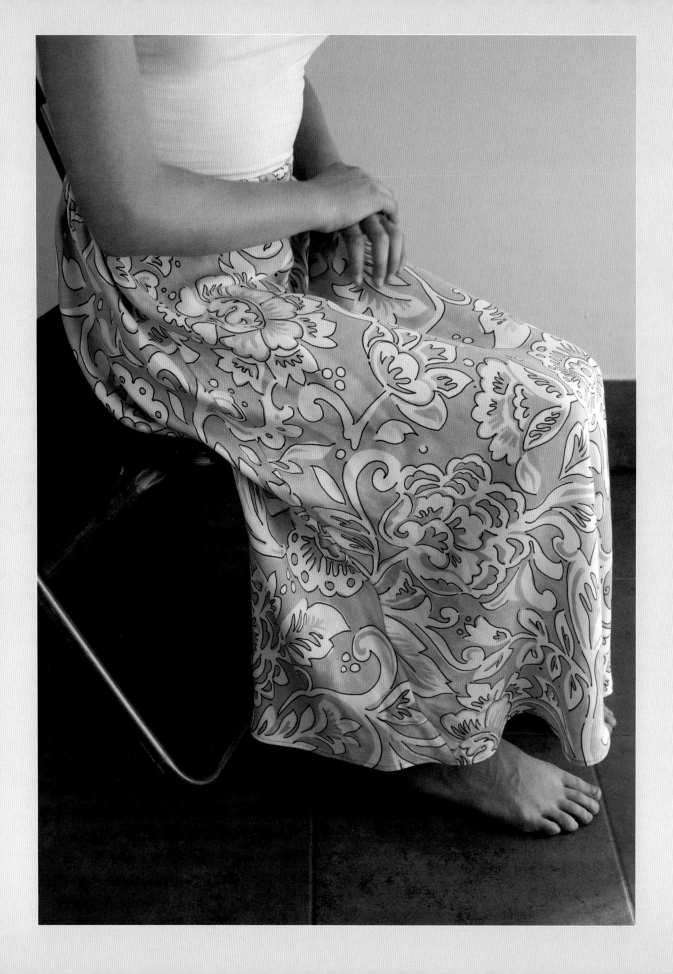

PROJECT 8

LEVELLING A SKIRT HEM

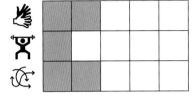

When you are in a seated position, you will notice that hem lengths change: they become longer at the back and shorter at the front. This can be a problem if you're a wheelchair user. Levelling off a seated skirt hem is a great way to create hems that work for being in a seated position. This project, however, can be applied to any skirt hem in any situation. If you experience curvature of the spine, have legs of differing lengths, have a twisted pelvis due to carrying heavy bags, or children, on one side – all these factors and more can affect how level our bodies are. It's a fact that no one is entirely symmetrical, so being able to level a hem to make it work for you can really change your wardrobe.

When pinning your hem, you may find it easier to pin in quarters, then eighths, and then any increments in between to get a level finish.

What you will need:

- A full-length skirt
- Someone to help pin your hem (optional)
- Safety pins
- Iron and ironing board, or similar
- Tape measure (optional)
- Fabric shears or rotary cutter and cutting mat
- Straight pins or fabric clips
- Sewing machine
- Matching sewing thread

1. Put on your skirt and sit how you will be seated while wearing it.

2. If you can, ask a friend or family member to help you pin the hem, as this will make achieving a level finish

much easier. Bending down causes the hem to drop, making it harder to get an accurate measurement. Try to keep yourself upright and looking forwards, if you are able to, as this will help keep

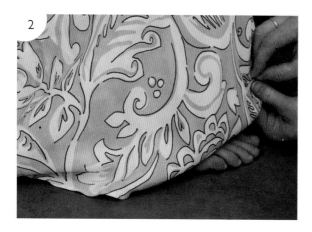

the hem still while being pinned. Start at the centre front of the hem. Fold the hem fabric under until you find the length you want. Secure it with a safety pin. This is the point you will work from for the rest of the hem.

3. Work your way around the skirt hem following the same process, folding up the fabric and pinning the new length. As you do this, keep an eye on the hem to make sure the front, back and sides all sit level.

4. Pin all the way round, checking the length as you go. Adjust the safety pins if required. Use as many safety pins as needed, pinning regularly, as this will make it easier when you take the skirt off. Do take as long as you need with this step. It's the most important stage so don't hurry, and make sure you are happy before removing the skirt.

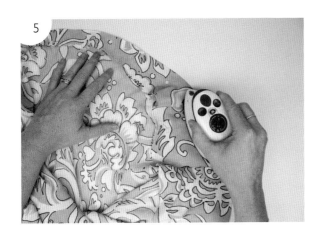

5. Lay the skirt flat on your ironing board or mat and press the hem. You can use a tape measure to check the hem depths are equal if you wish but, as this is an alteration based on levelling a hem according to the body's needs, accurate pinning in the early steps should avoid any requirement for this. As you press, allow the fabric to form a smooth curve. You may need to make tiny adjustments to the pins to allow this to happen.

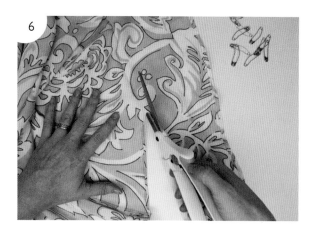

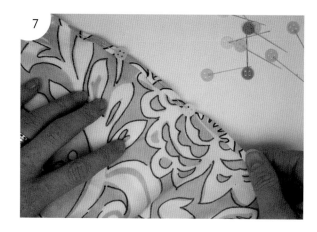

6. Remove the safety pins and, using your fabric shears or rotary cutter, trim away the excess hem 1cm (⅜") below the crease line you have just pressed into the fabric.

7. Create a roll hem around the edge of the hem and pin or clip in place using straight pins or fabric clips, whichever you prefer. To make a roll hem, fold the fabric beneath the crease in half (so that the raw edge sits

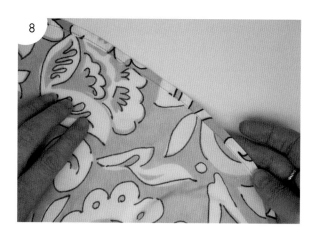

in the ironed crease), then fold again at the crease point. This will give you a neat 0.5cm (¼") hem with the raw edge enclosed. Repeat this process round the whole hem. You may wish to try the skirt on again at this point to make sure you are happy with the length before stitching it down.

8. Edge stitch the hem down along the top edge of the roll hem all the way round. Give the new hem a press to complete your skirt.

Top Tips

» If having someone to help pin your hem is not something you can arrange, it is possible to pin your own hem. However, bending down to pin, sitting or standing up straight again to assess, and adjusting the pins as required in front of a full-length mirror is a very trial and error way of completing this step. It is manageable but be aware this process can be challenging on energy levels. Alternatively, a chalk hem marker can help you measure your own hems.

» I recommend using safety pins as opposed to straight pins when pinning up your hem. Straight pins can fall out when the garment is moved around, put on and taken off. They can also be painful if they catch the skin. Safety pins stay put and are safer to use. Fabric clips can also be used but bear in mind these will only hold the lower fold. If you are taking up large amounts of fabric, clips won't prevent the fabric from flapping down, making it harder to assess the finished length.

» When pinning your hem, you may find it easier to pin in quarters, then eighths, and then any increments in between to get a level finish.

PROJECT 9

REPOSITIONING POCKETS

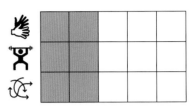

If you are a wheelchair user, or spend a lot of your time sitting down, pockets on the back of trousers are, at best, a little redundant and, at worst, a painful health hazard. Removing them is a good means of making trousers more accessible. Repurposing those pockets is then a great way to be resourceful and can also improve the design of the trousers. Traditional hip pockets on trousers are mostly pointless for a wheelchair user to have on their garment. In this project, we remove the back pockets and reposition them on the thigh, making the trousers far more practical. Even if you aren't a wheelchair user, this is a wonderful idea for upcycling an old pair of trousers and creating a fun design feature.

Why not remake the pockets from a contrasting fabric to turn them into an eye-catching feature?

What you will need:

- A pair of trousers with top stitched back pockets
- Stitch ripper, small embroidery scissors or snips
- Straight pins or fabric basting glue
- Sewing machine
- Matching sewing thread

1. Check that the pockets on the back of your trousers are top stitched and don't have any rivets or metalwork on them. See Top Tips for what to do if they do have rivets or metalwork.

2. Using a stitch ripper or your tool of choice, remove the pockets from the back of the trousers.

3. Decide where you would like the pockets to go on the legs of the trousers. Pin them in place using straight pins or fabric basting glue.

4. Unpick the side seam of the first trouser leg up to around 2.5cm (1") below the bottom of the pinned pocket. This will open up the leg and make it easier to reach the pocket for stitching.

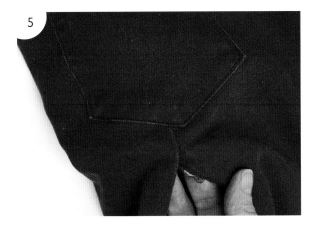

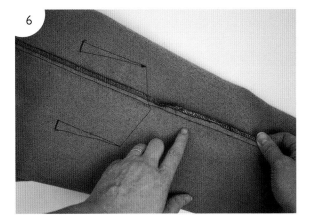

5. Top stitch the pocket in place following the same stitch lines as were used originally.

6. Turn the trouser leg inside out and stitch the side seam back together. Finish the raw edge with an overlocker, overcasting stitch or zigzag stitch on your sewing machine, if needed. Repeat on the second leg to complete your project.

Top Tips

» If your trouser pockets do have rivets or metalwork on them, these can be removed using a specialist tool. Use your preferred search engine to find videos on how this can be done. It's also a great thing to do to improve the comfort of your trousers if you wear them while seated for long periods of time.

» Why not remake the pockets from a contrasting fabric to turn them into an eye-catching feature?

» Reproducing the original lines of stitching when you're doing alterations helps give the garment a professional finish.

PROJECT 10

REMOVING EXCESS FABRIC FROM SEATED TROUSERS

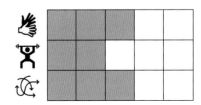

Trousers feature in most wardrobes and, for many people, are a comfortable and versatile garment to wear. However, when we sit in trousers, the way they interact with our bodies changes and, for a wheelchair user, or someone who sits for the majority of the time, this can cause discomfort or even health challenges. One of these changes is in the distribution of fabric at the hip bend and behind the knees. In this project, we reshape the sides of a pair of trousers to remove some of this excess, making the trousers far more comfortable to wear in a seated position. This can benefit those who drive for a living or sit at a desk for long periods of time. In fact, anybody who sits more than they stand could find these adjustments beneficial.

I recommend using safety pins instead of straight pins when marking your knee and hip points, as they won't fall out when you're putting on the trousers and taking them off.

What you will need:

- A pair of trousers
- Safety pins
- Stitch ripper or snips
- Tape measure
- Ruler
- Fabric pen or chalk marker
- Iron and ironing board, or similar
- Fabric shears or rotary cutter and cutting mat
- Straight pins or fabric clips
- Sewing machine
- Matching sewing thread

1. Put on your trousers and, using a safety pin, mark the point at which your knee bends. Pin both sides of the knee: one pin on the outside side seam and one on the inside leg seam. If both legs need to be altered, repeat this process with the second leg.

2. Add another safety pin to the side seam of the trousers at the point where the hip bends. Remove the trousers.

3. In this image, you can clearly see the positions of the safety pins once the trousers have been removed.

4. Using a stitch ripper, or tool of your choice, unpick the inside leg seam from the hem up to around 7.5cm (3") past the safety pin at the knee.

5. Repeat this process, unpicking the outside side seam and this time working from the hem, past the safety pin at the knee, up to approximately 7.5cm (3") past the safety pin at the hip.

6. Lay the trousers flat on your work surface so you're looking at the front. Using your fabric marker of choice, mark the points at the knee where you placed your safety pins. Then, with a tape measure or ruler, mark points

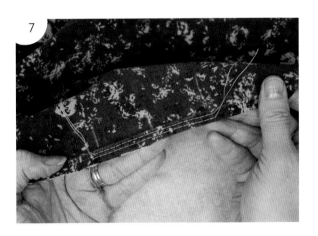

4cm (1 ¾") either side of this central pin mark. Repeat for both sides of the knee. Remove the safety pins.

7. Next, you will need to create gathering stitches between these marks. To do this, set your sewing machine stitch length to its longest.

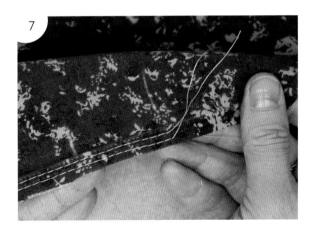

This is usually 5. Making sure you have long ends on both your top and bobbin threads, stitch two parallel lines of stitching from one mark to the other, cutting the threads with long tails at the end.

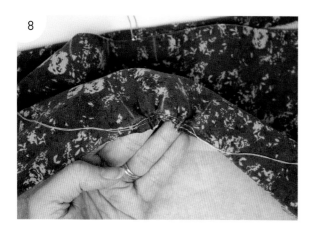

8. Gripping the long threads on the top of the fabric at one end, pull gently. The fabric will start to gather up. Don't pull too hard as the threads could snap or pull all the way through.

If this happens, you'll need to start the process again. Repeat this step for both sides of the knee.

9. Turn the trousers over so you're now looking at the back. At the hips, using a fabric marker, make a mark

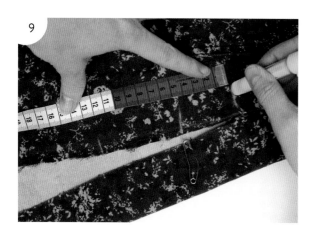

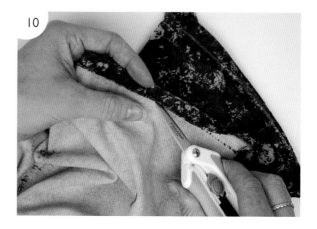

at the point where the safety pin sits, in the same way as you did for the knees. With your tape measure or ruler, make another mark 5cm (2") above this central point (towards the waistband), and a mark 7cm (2¾") below it (towards the hem). Sew your

gathering stitches between these two marks and gather up the fabric, as you did in steps 7 and 8.

10. Using a stitch ripper, or tool of your choice, unpick the hem of the trouser leg.

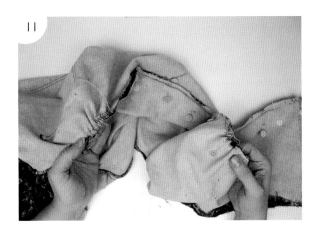

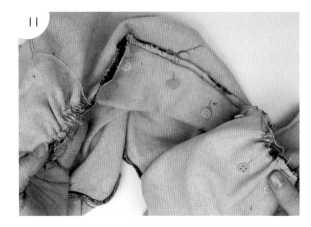

11. Line up your side seams with the gathered sections and, using straight pins or fabric clips, pin or clip the two seams together. Stitch them closed, following the original seam line. At the points of gathering, sew over the gathers to secure them. If any of the gathering stitches are showing on the outside of the trousers once you have sewn up these seams, you can remove them.

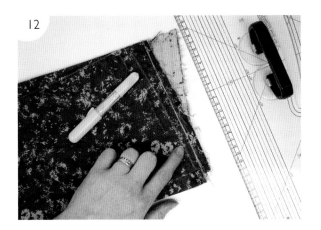

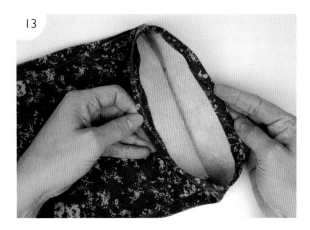

12. The hem will most likely now look very uneven as we have altered the distribution of fabric in the trouser leg. Using your ruler and fabric marker, square off the hem of the trouser leg, making sure it is square to the central line of the trousers. (Imagine a straight line running through the middle of the trouser leg – your hem needs to be at right angles to this.) Cut away any excess.

13. Finish your hem by turning it up 1cm (⅜"), then 1cm (⅜") again. Top stitch around the hem to secure it in place.

14. Press your seams and your hem. The gather on the hip should sit on the back part of the trousers while the front is flat. This will allow for more fabric to accommodate the curve of the seat, while reducing the fabric in the crease at the top of the legs.

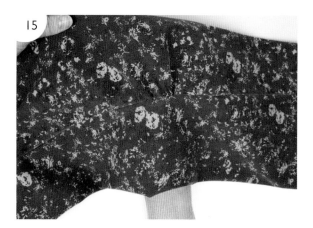

15. The gathers at the knee should sit on the front side of the trouser leg. This allows for more fabric to accommodate the bent knee and reduces the amount of excess fabric behind the knee.

16. Repeat these steps for the second leg if required.

Top Tips

» Altering your trousers in this way can affect the finished length. If your trousers don't have any excess length in them to begin with, there is a chance they will now be too short. You can either turn them into capri pants or wear them as a cropped style. Alternatively, you could use the "Lengthening and Shortening Jeans" project on page 89 to add some length to the finished pair.

» When you are marking your hem, you may find it beneficial to try on the trousers before sewing, to get an accurate length. Just as with skirts, trouser hems can dip at the back and sit shorter at the front. Why not follow the "Levelling a Skirt Hem" project on page 97 to mark your trouser hems so they sit level for you.

» I recommend using safety pins instead of straight pins when marking your knee and hip points, as they won't fall out when you're putting on the trousers and taking them off.

Amber Brown

Amber started sewing when they were twelve years old, after their grandmother taught them how to make their own clothing. They were diagnosed as autistic and ADHD as a child and have gone on to be diagnosed with a heart condition, Ehlers Danlos and hypersomnia. Living in Arizona, USA, they were adapting their clothing to suit their needs long before accessible fashion had a name.

"Give yourself the grace and space to create at your own level. Invariably with a disability, you're already working below what is considered the starting line; already fighting obstacles others are not, in order to accomplish the same result. The end result doesn't matter — no one will notice if your hem is a little wonky or the sleeve is crooked. Focus on making clothes that are comfortable and functional rather than clothes that don't look handmade."

HOW DID YOU GET INTO SEWING?

My grandmother sewed all the time, making church robes and fancy gowns. When I'd go to stay with her, she would be sewing so I had no choice but to sit and sew with her. She told me she wasn't going to buy me any clothes and instead taught me how to make my own. It was about this time that I started to recognise my sensory issues around clothing. My dad was a military man and didn't really know how to dress me when I was a child, so I spent most of my early childhood running around in tracksuits and sweatpants. As I started to come into my own sense of style, I began to realise how much I hated the way certain clothes and fabrics felt on my body. They were too tight or the seams were too bulky; the fabric didn't breathe or didn't move right. I found myself mostly wearing clothes designed for little boys as these felt softer and more comfortable. However, I really liked traditionally girlie things and sparkly dresses, so I started adapting my clothes right at the beginning of my sewing journey.

Back then, I didn't really understand why I found certain things uncomfortable; I just knew I hated the way serger seams felt against my skin, for example. My grandma taught me how to make French seams on everything I made, which I found much more comfortable.

I sewed from around ages twelve to twenty, on and off. Then I was pulled away from my sewing with work. I also received several other diagnoses around this time. I went through cancer and was diagnosed with hypersomnia too, which is classified as excessive daytime sleepiness, verging on narcolepsy. At one point, I was sleeping around eighteen hours a day and this had a huge impact on my work and sewing. It would take me weeks to complete small projects as I would literally fall asleep at my sewing machine. Simple steps like cutting out would take all the energy I had for the day. Hypersomnia can also cause memory issues, meaning I would often forget where I was in a project. To accommodate this, I kept a notebook in which I would note down each step as I completed it, for example, "sewn on pockets". This meant if I did fall asleep, I would still be able to find where I was up to.

My health is fairly well managed now so I'm more able to get back into sewing. However, my disabilities still affect me every day and I've made adjustments to my work space which enable me to take on bigger projects. Managing my energy levels is my main focus so I take a lot of breaks. My hands can cramp a great deal and I have to take care when cutting out patterns and fabric. I also do little, if any, hand sewing. My grandmother would roll in her grave if she knew how little hand sewing I do!

Something else I find beneficial is to break down tasks into smaller parts. An example of this would be threading elastic through a channel. The gripping and pulling motion involved in this often leaves my hands numb and cramping. To feed elastic through a channel traditionally, a safety pin, or similar, is attached to one end and passed into one end of the fabric channel. The pin is then pulled through the channel, bit by bit, by feel until it emerges through the other side. This involves a lot of gripping and pulling and puts strain on my hands, often leaving them numb and cramping. To help me manage, instead of feeding the elastic through the whole waistband in one go, I will break it down into two parts: the front and then the back. Although this is effectively making it a bigger job, it allows my hands the breaks they need to be able to continue working afterwards.

WHAT CHALLENGES HAVE YOU FACED WITH ACCESSING THE CRAFT?

My biggest hurdle with accessing sewing has been my sensory issues. I've realised I must feel a fabric before I can commit to sewing a garment from it. Accessing fabric stores where I live is challenging. We have a couple fairly nearby but if I need to go elsewhere, the next closest fabric store is a six-hour drive away. If I'm visiting that store, it's with a shopping list and a budget; I can't just pop down there on a whim.

Online fabric shopping has been one of the biggest blocks to my sewing journey. Online orders, once cut, cannot be returned, and I've received fabrics and known instantly that there's no way I can tolerate wearing them. I have a rubber bucket in my closet that's marked "sell or gift" and any mis-purchased fabrics end up in there. It's very frustrating. I like to support small businesses but they don't tend to offer a sample cutting service. I generally order the smallest increment I can, usually a fat quarter, which I often then use on small projects such as pockets, facings, masks, or I'll put them in a quilt so they don't go to waste.

"You do not need to sew to couture standards for your garment to be acceptable to wear."

Occasionally, I'll find a fabric online that I love the look of but there will only be a few metres left. In these instances, I'll order it and run the risk of it not being suitable. If it isn't right, it goes in the rehoming bucket. I do have certain "safe" fabrics from different vendors that I know I can buy, and they will always be perfect for me. For example, I really cannot tolerate pure linen against my skin. However, there is one store that sells softened linen and I know I can use this with no problems.

Outside of fabric, my biggest challenge is my ability to sustain my energy levels and concentration. I get tired easily and I'm also very easily distracted. I always have piles of projects in progress, all at different stages, and I jump from one to another.

The biggest drain on my energy levels is the cutting process. I feel that modern commercial patterns aren't overly accessible as they count on you being precise. This can be difficult for people with mobility or dexterity issues. A PDF pattern will require printing, taping, cutting, pinning, and the fabric cutting, even before you start sewing, and I find this process exhausting.

I live with my dad as his carer and my sewing space is in my bedroom. When you're working in a small space, you are often reliant on laying out patterns and fabric on the floor, or dining-room table, or kitchen counter. I cut out on my bedroom floor. However, my Ehlers Danlos means I can dislocate my joints very easily, so I find getting down on the floor and then up again challenging. Often, also, after preparing and cutting a pattern on the floor, I will need to put myself in braces, with no energy left to sew anything. My niece often asks me to make things for her so, in return, I ask her to do my cutting-out for me. She now buys her own fabric and cuts out the pattern pieces at home before bringing them to me.

I've made a large number of modifications to my sewing space to accommodate both my access needs and the size of area I have to sew in. As my sewing room is also my bedroom, I've opted to have a smaller bed so that I can maximise my available floor space. I have shelves at different heights all around the room so, whether I'm standing, seated, or kneeling on the floor, I can access the tools I need. I also now have a rolling cart with four shelves that I can wheel to where I need it. The shelves aren't organised but I know what's on each one and this system works for me.

I use an ironing pad rather than an ironing board as this means I can either iron on the floor or seated at a table. Pressing is then much more accessible for me, and I can achieve a lot more with the energy I have by keeping everything within easy reach.

WHAT CHALLENGES DO YOU HAVE WITH CLOTHING?

I'm a plus-size woman and I find the options I have available to me when I buy from shops are usually made from cheap, thin polyester, put together with quick serger seams. Bought clothes also seem to have lots of closures: buttons, zippers and so on. I can't have zippers at the back as reaching round to fasten them would cause me to faint. I do find

closures very challenging generally, because of the dexterity they require. It's a reason I avoid pants. Not only do I hate the feel of wearing them, I can never be sure I'm going to be able to manage the closures. It's one thing to discover your hands can't grasp a zipper at home; it's another to find this in a restroom when you're out and, suddenly, you're having to ask strangers to help you undo your pants! I find it much easier to get into and out of skirts and dresses, so I tend to wear these most of the time.

I avoid clothing that takes a lot of energy to get into and out of, such as bodysuits and jumpsuits. If I have to expend precious energy dressing myself, I'll no longer have the energy to do the task I left the house to do.

To be honest, I don't do a lot of clothes shopping anymore. I've developed a unique style and to accommodate that, I need to make most of my clothes myself. If I do find something in the shops

> *"I recommend making yourself a fitting shell or bodice block. This is a simple pattern shape that forms the basis for your shape and can be adapted to make anything you want."*

I like, I'll purchase it in several different colours and will often take a pattern from it so I can reproduce it myself. I need my clothes to not be too clingy but to fit me nicely. I can't have scratchy labels and the fabric needs to be soft. I hate to wear sleeves too, so tops need to not be tight around the armholes. If there are serger seams – the thing that affects me the most – I've learned to just top stitch them flat so they don't rub against my skin.

I've discovered a lot of ways to work around the things I don't like about clothing. My grandmother noticed I was unable to manage buttons or zippers, so taught me how to insert snap tape, making garments much easier to put on and take off. She also showed me how to replace a zip fastening on a fitted dress with just one hook and eye, or create a tie-on fastening. I don't want to have to rely on other people to help me get dressed.

ANY TIPS OR ADVICE?

My main piece of advice would be not to try to do everything at once. Have

"I buy cheap bed sheets from charity shops or fabric from discount bins and make a basic version of the garment. This way I can check the feel of it on my body and if it needs adjusting anywhere."

a sewing notebook with you and write out all the steps you need to do for your project. Then just focus on one or two steps at a time. Knowing you can take breaks in between steps is also important. Unless you are on a deadline, such as an upcoming special occasion or similar, you can take as long as you need to achieve your final goal.

You don't need to sew to couture standards for your garment to be acceptable to wear. I can't hand finish my garments and, for a long time, I decided my clothes didn't look good enough because of this. Now I use a contrast colour top thread on all my hems and cuffs to make a feature of the fact that I top stitch everything I make. I've also made accommodations to garments by choosing not to add in the sleeves and for a long time I was concerned this meant my makes just didn't look right. However, the most important thing is that your garment fits you well and is comfortable. It doesn't need to be finished perfectly to be valid. Don't be afraid to take those shortcuts if it means your sewing process is easier for you.

When you're choosing what to sew, don't pick something because it's the trendy thing everyone seems to be making. Make things that are already in your wardrobe that you know work for you.

The best piece of advice I can give comes from my grandmother. Remember, when you're disabled, you can't move your body in the same way others can. This means that fitting your garments and taking your own measurements will be more challenging. If you can ask someone else to measure you, do so, or just do your best with what you have.

I recommend making yourself a fitting shell or bodice block. This is a simple pattern shape that forms the basis for your shape and can be adapted to make anything you want. You can incorporate all your own needs and accommodations so you know that anything you want to make will fit you exactly as you need it to. My shells have the darts in the right place for me, and there is excess at the sides to accommodate a snap tape or hook-and-loop tape fastening. I have also made them so the fit is slightly loose, which is how I like my clothes to fit. Commercial patterns often need a certain level of adapting and, although the process of creating the bodice blocks takes a little additional learning and effort in the first place, in the long run it removes the need to adapt patterns over and over again, and can ease the mental burden when you may already be struggling with other things.

If you have fluctuating energy levels, you can learn a lot about pattern drafting from books, which can be read when you don't have the energy or capacity to sew. You can grow your knowledge and understanding around it without needing to do any physical movements.

My bodice blocks are cut from poster board so they won't disintegrate or tear. I store them behind my bookshelf, ready for when I start a new project. You can make blocks for all sorts of garments. This can be done with commercial patterns too. If you find a pattern for something that works for you, copy it onto poster

Amber's Top Tips

1. Maximise your sewing space and make everything accessible by having shelves set at different heights, and keeping your equipment on a rolling trolley.

2. Keep a sewing notebook so you can break down projects into smaller steps and keep track of your progress.

3. Feel your fabrics before buying them whenever you can to avoid costly wastage, and make sure they feel nice against your skin.

4. Make yourself a bodice block that contains your adaptations, or transfer successful patterns to poster board so you can reuse them over and over.

5. A gardening kneeling pad and a portable ironing pad can help if you're having to work on the floor.

board and keep it forever. With any sort of disability, finding things that work for you can be really challenging. Once you find that thing, you don't want to risk the company discontinuing it, or losing pattern pieces, or having them tear.

The real secret to my success is that I make toiles, or mock-ups, of everything I make. It may seem like a waste of energy but it pays off in the long run. I buy cheap bed sheets from charity shops or fabric from discount bins and make a basic version of the garment. This way I can check the feel of it on my body and if it needs adjusting anywhere. I use French seams in all my projects, so mocking up my garment also enables me to see that the pattern will accommodate this.

Access to sewing for me has always been about managing my time and energy; having a sewing space with tools that help support me is key. I have a large cutting mat on the floor and use a rotary cutter to cut my fabric. I'm quite new to rotary cutters and I'm not very good with it yet, but I don't believe

> "The real secret to my success is that I make toiles, or mock-ups, of everything I make. It may seem like a waste of energy but it pays off in the long run."

everything has to be done perfectly. I use a gardening knee pad when I'm on the floor. This has saved me a great deal of knee, hip and back pain which, in turn, helps me to sew for longer.

I also use a headlamp when I'm sewing. My room is quite dark, but that aside, it helps me see my straight pins more easily, and concentrate when I'm looking at patterns.

I wear fingerless compression gloves when I'm sewing too. They're thin, allowing me to still feel the fabric, but I find they help keep the blood flowing around my hands. Another hack is to use a temporary basting spray on my fabrics to fix my pattern pieces in place. This means I don't need to struggle with straight pins. I simply spray the fabric, apply my pattern pieces, and cut the shapes out before removing the pattern pieces.

A tool I've recently added to my sewing kit is a fabric notcher. My hands can get shaky and trying to cut notches in fabric can be challenging. Often I've avoided cutting them. The notcher helps enormously and means I can cut my notches more easily and accurately.

With fabrics, I always try to avoid polyester. I just find it doesn't breathe well and, as I overheat very easily, I aim to use natural fibres. Textures of fabrics are important to me. A good alternative I often use is lyocell as it's a natural fibre and beautifully comfortable to wear.

I also use and wear a lot of cotton sateen. This is a dressier fabric and has some stretch to it as well. My most used fabric is cotton. I especially love to dress make with quilting cotton. It seems to get softer the more it's washed, and it holds up well because it's designed to exist in a quilt for a very long time. It's also generally thinner, which means it can be easier to French seam.

Just start sewing. It doesn't matter how bad it is – you will feel so accomplished completing your first make. You will also learn so much about the sort of things you want to create. If it doesn't work out, it's ok. Repetition is the key to learning! Allow yourself to mess it up; take as much time as you need to. As long as you love it on your body, that's all that matters.

Meet the Maker
Favourite Tools

1. BASTING SPRAY
2. NOTCHER
3. IRONING PAD

Amber Brown
You can find Amber on tiktok @weplayindreams

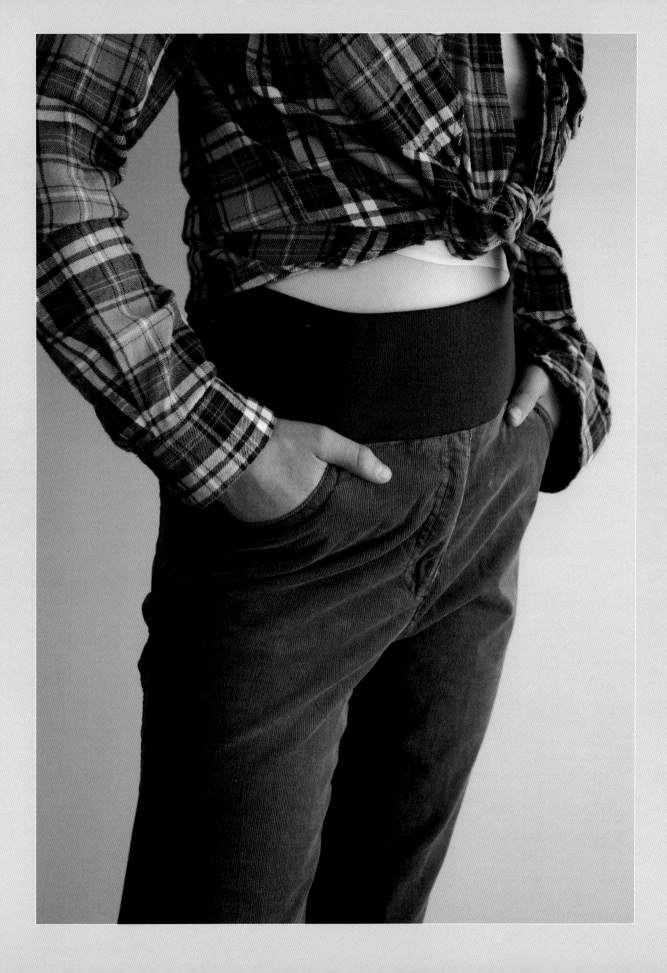

PROJECT 11

STRETCH WAISTBAND

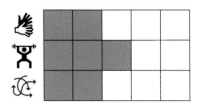

This is an alteration to make everybody happy. Whether you have a stoma or nephrostomy bag, a catheter, diabetic pump, feeding tube, sensory issues around tight waistbands, dexterity issues with button fastenings, experience bloating through IBS or menopause, are pregnant, find your waist size fluctuates throughout the day – or you just really enjoy the comfort of an elasticated waistband – this project truly is All Access!

If you're making maternity trousers or skirts, try using lycra or jersey for a wider band, if you wish the band to reach over your bump entirely.

What you will need:

- A pair of trousers or a skirt
- Stitch ripper or tool or your choice
- Tape measure
- Ribbing 20cm (8") wide, to the circumference of your trouser waistband
- 2.5cm (1") wide elastic to the circumference of your waist
- Straight pins or fabric clips
- Fabric scissors, or rotary cutter and cutting mat
- An overlocker, or sewing machine capable of doing a stretch stitch
- Matching sewing thread

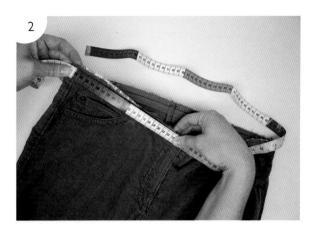

1. Using a stitch ripper, or tool of your choice, unpick and remove the waistband from your trousers.

2. With a tape measure, measure the circumference of the top of the trousers. In this example, mine measures 90cm (36").

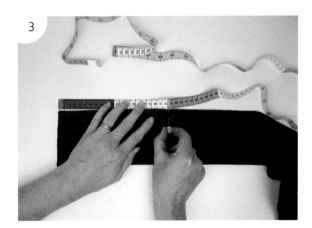

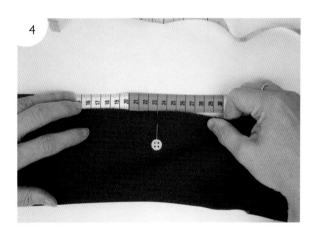

3. To create the new stretch waistband, you will need to calculate the amount of stretch in your ribbing. Mark 20cm on your ribbing with a straight pin (I recommend doing this in cm for greater accuracy, although you can use inches if you prefer).

4. Holding the end at zero, gently pull the pinned end along the tape measure until the easy stretch stops (you want to calculate the natural ease, not over-stretch your ribbing). Note where the pin sits now. In this example, my pin moves from 20cm to 23cm, meaning I have 3cm stretch in my ribbing.

Use this equation to calculate your amount of stretch:

Equation	Measurements for my trousers
20cm divided by stretched measurement	20 divided by 23 = 0.87
Total waistband circumference x this number	90cm x 0.87 = 78.3
This number + 2cm for seam allowance	78.3 + 2 = 80.3cm

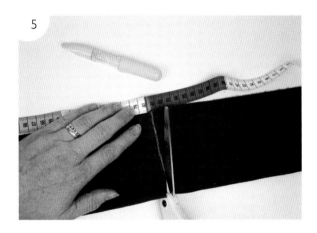

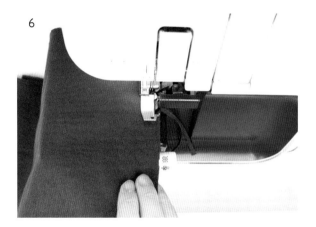

5. Cut your ribbing to the new length you have just calculated.

6. Open out the ribbing so it lies flat. Using an overlocker, or stretch stitch on your sewing machine, sew the two short ends together to make a complete circle.

7. Fold the ribbing in half lengthways, enclosing the overlocked seam inside. [No pic]

Top Tip!

Use this calculation method when working with stretch fabrics that need to be tight to the body, to remove the stretch excess from your pattern.

8. Cut a length of elastic that fits comfortably around your waist. Overlap the two ends by 1cm (⅜") and stitch together using a wide zigzag stitch.

9. Insert the elastic inside the folded ribbing so that it sits up against the folded edge. If it helps, pin the elastic in place to prevent it from slipping or moving. Make sure that the join in the elastic is in a different place to the join

in the ribbing. This will prevent bulkiness and potential discomfort when worn.

10. Measure and mark the quarter points around the waistband. An optional extra here is to top stitch the elastic in place using a stretch stitch.

This will help prevent the elastic twisting inside the ribbing, keeping it nice and flat.

11. Mark the quarter points on the top edge of your trousers or skirt.

12. Line these up with the quarter points on the waistband. With right sides together, pin the waistband in place at these 4 points. The ribbing waistband should be smaller than the waistband of your trousers.

13. Stitch the ribbing to the top of your skirt or trousers, using a regular straight stitch, stretching the ribbing to fit as you go. You can oversew this line of stitching a couple of times for additional security if you wish.

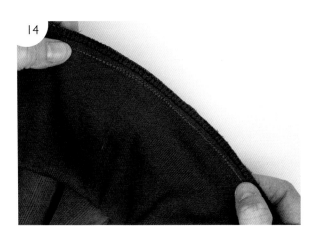

14. Use your overlocker, an overcasting stitch or zigzag stitch to neaten the raw edge.

15. Turn the waistband up and press. Stitch a line of topstitching just below where the waistband meets the trousers, catching down the seam for additional strength.

16. Your new stretch waistband is now complete.

Top Tips

» If you're making maternity trousers or skirts, try using lycra or jersey for a wider band, if you wish the band to reach over your bump entirely.

» Why not use a fun colour ribbing as a bold and stylish design choice!

» If you want to add a drawstring, stitch small buttonholes into the front of the ribbing before folding in half, and skip the top stitching in step 10.

PROJECT 12

SENSORY SEAMS TWO WAYS

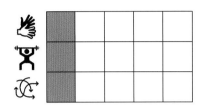

If you find seams uncomfortable, scratchy or irritating, either due to sensory issues or delicate skin, this is the project for you. These are also good techniques for strengthening your seams to make your garment last longer. Great for your wallet, and for the environment too!

The closer to the edge of the tape you can stitch your lines of edge stitching, the more comfortable the seams will be to wear, as there won't be any edges protruding to cause irritation.

What you will need:

- Any clothing with scratchy seams
- Cotton twill tape
- Straight pins or fabric basting glue
- Small fabric scissors or snips
- Sewing machine
- Matching sewing thread

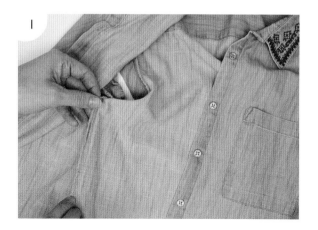

Method 1:

1. Look inside your garment and identify the seams that are uncomfortable. Cut lengths of cotton twill tape long enough to cover the full length of the seams, plus some extra at the top and bottom.

2. Turn under one end of the cotton twill tape and position it at the top of the seam. Using your straight pins or fabric basting glue, secure the tape in place, making sure the seam allowance underneath sits flat under the tape.

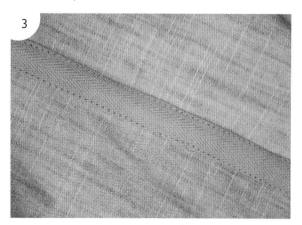

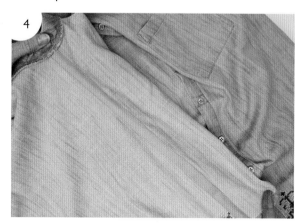

3. Edge stitch the tape in place down both sides, enclosing the seam underneath. These lines of stitching will be visible from the outside of the garment.

4. Making sure both ends of the tape are tucked under as you stitch round will secure them and stop any fraying. Stitching along the top and bottom edges of the tape, as well as down the sides, will further help to secure the tape in place.

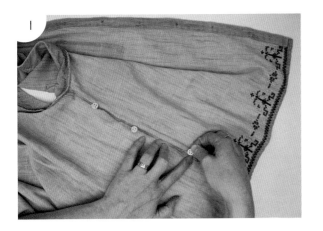

Method 2:

1. Using your straight pins or fabric basting glue, secure the seam down to the body of the garment, making sure it lies flat.

2. Edge stitch the seam allowance down to the body of the garment, as close to the edge as you can. This will create a line of visible stitching on the outside of the garment.

Top Tips

» For covering curved seams, such as armholes or princess seams, use bias binding tape instead of cotton twill tape, as this will curve with the seam.

» The closer to the edge of the tape you can stitch your lines of edge stitching, the more comfortable the seams will be to wear, as there won't be any edges protruding to cause irritation.

» If you are making your garment from a pattern, consider using run and fell seams or French seams to make the seams more comfortable against the skin.

PROJECT 13

LOOSENING TIGHT SLEEVES

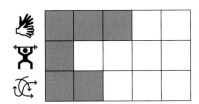

Tight sleeves are a real sensory no-no for me, so this was one of the first alterations I started making to my own clothes. It's great for creating looser, more flowing sleeves from the sleeves already on your garment, and it has a plethora of applications. This is a great adaptation if you experience lymphodema, or general swelling in your arms, if you find putting sleeved garments on challenging, or if you need easier access to your arms for medical treatment. And from a style perspective, a floaty sleeve is beautiful. This can be a great upcycling alteration to an old, outdated garment.

If you don't have a curved ruler, or find using rulers difficult, why not cut a curved template from paper, or use the edge of a plate or bowl to mark your curve.

What you will need:

- A top with sleeves
- Stitch ripper, or tool of your choice
- Fabric pen or chalk pencil
- Fabric scissors
- Curved ruler
- Bias binding
- Straight pins or fabric clips
- Sewing machine
- Matching sewing thread
- Iron and ironing board, or similar

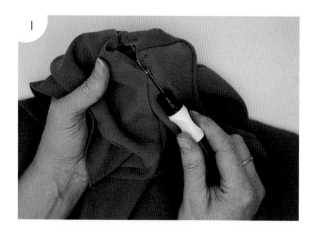

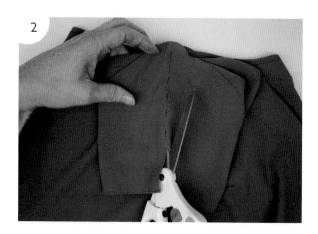

1. Using a stitch ripper, or tool of your choice, unpick the sleeve of your garment along the sleeve head seam. Don't unpick the whole sleeve, just enough to be able to access it. Around 12cm (4¾") should be plenty.

2. Mark a line down the centre of the sleeve, from sleeve head to cuff, using your fabric pen or chalk pencil. With your shears, cut along this line, opening up the sleeve.

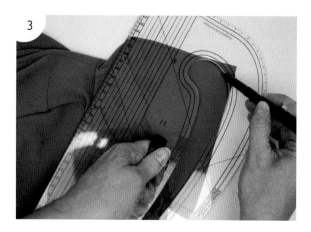

3. Using a curved ruler and your fabric marker, mark a curved edge to one of the cuff corners you have just created.

4. Cut along the curved line you have just drawn. Lay this over the other side of the cuff and use the cut curve as a template to mark the shape. This will help make sure both sides are symmetrical.

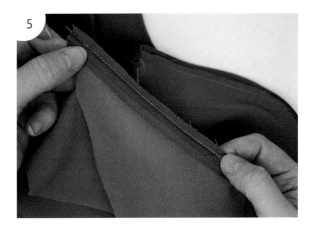

5. Open one side of your bias binding tape and lay it along the raw cut edge, on the right side of the fabric, down the centre of your sleeve. Pin or clip in place. Stitch along the fold groove, attaching the tape from the

sleeve head (on one side), down the sleeve and around your curved corner, along the cuff edge, round the second curved corner, and up the sleeve to the sleeve head on the other side.

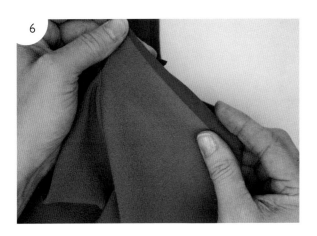

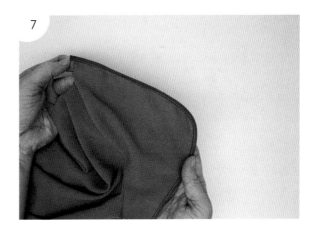

6. Fold the bias binding tape over to the inside of the sleeve, encasing the raw edges. Pin or clip in place.

7. Edge stitch along the edge of the folded bias binding tape from the inside of the sleeve, securing it in place. If you prefer, and are able, you can hand sew this edge down.

8. Reposition the bound edges of the slit sleeve into the armhole of the top. Stitch closed the seam you originally unpicked in step 1. Use an overcasting stitch or zigzag stitch to neaten the raw edge.

9. Give your new split sleeve a press and your top is ready to wear.

Top Tips

» If you don't have a curved ruler, or find using rulers difficult, why not cut a curved template from paper, or use the edge of a plate or bowl to mark your curve.

» Use a narrow bias binding tape if your fabric is delicate, and a wider tape if it's heavier or you want to make more of a statement sleeve.

» If you are more experienced, you can set your overlocker to a narrow roll hem and use this to edge your sleeve instead. This will give a wavy finish to the fabric border.

PROJECT 14

WIDENING A NECKLINE

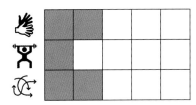

If you find tight necklines uncomfortable, this project will improve the feel of your clothes. It's a great one for creating easier access to the throat and neck, or a chest port, or if you just prefer a wider neckline. This is also a fantastic way to repair a garment that has damage to the neckline, or it can make a good upcycling project.

If you want to widen a neckline on a top that isn't made from a stretch fabric, consider using bias binding to edge the fabric, or to create a narrow facing along the new neckline.

What you will need:

- A jersey top
- Tape measure
- Fabric pen or chalk pencil
- Straight pins or fabric clips
- Fabric scissors or rotary cutter and cutting mat
- Snips or a stitch ripper
- An overlocker, or sewing machine capable of doing a stretch stitch
- Matching sewing thread
- Twin needle (optional)
- Iron and ironing board, or similar

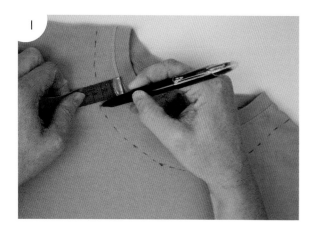

1. Using a tape measure to make sure your line is symmetrical and even, mark the widened neckline you want to achieve on the front of your top.

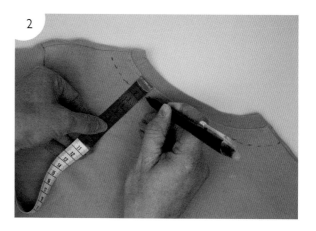

2. Repeat the process on the back. You may want to widen the neckline more at the front than at the back. Choose the new neckline that works for what you need.

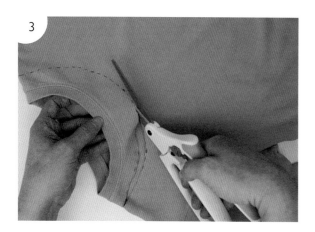

3. Cut along the line you have drawn, creating a new neckline edge.

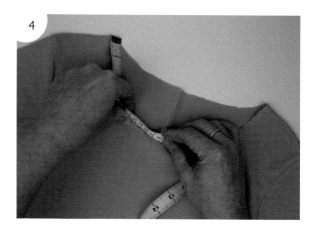

4. Measure the edge of the new neckline to determine the circumference.

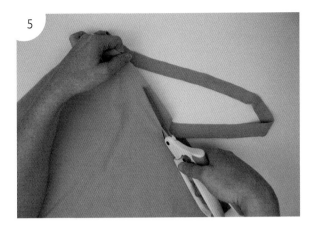

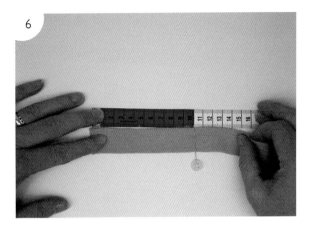

5. Using a pair of fabric shears or a rotary cutter, cut off the bottom hem of the top. Here, I have followed the top line of stitching as a guide. If you are shortening the body length, cut

away whatever you need minus 2cm (¾") to allow for hemming. This excess fabric will form the new neckline.

6. To create the new neckline, you will need to calculate the amount of stretch in your jersey. Mark 10cm on

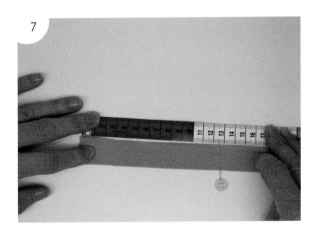

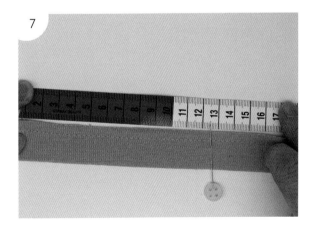

the removed hem strip with a straight pin. (I recommend doing this in cm for greater accuracy, although you can use inches if you prefer.)

7. Holding the end at zero, gently pull the pinned end along the tape measure until the easy stretch stops

(you want to calculate the natural ease, not over-stretch your jersey). Note where the pin sits now. In this example, my pin moves from 10cm to 12.5cm, meaning I have 2.5cm of stretch in my fabric.

Use this equation to calculate your amount of stretch:

Equation	Measurements for my new neckline
10cm divided by stretched measurement	10 divided by 12.5 = 0.8
Total circumference of new neckline x this number	60cm x 0.8 = 48
This number + 2cm for seam allowance	48 + 2 = 50cm

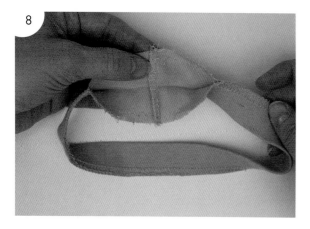

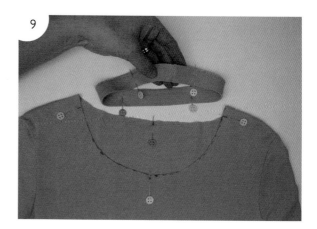

8. Cut your jersey hem piece to the new length you have just calculated. Using a stitch ripper or snips, open up any stitching that still remains in the hem strip. Then, you can open the ends so the fabric lies flat, and stitch them together to form a complete circle, using an overlocker, overcasting stitch or zigzag stitch.

9. Mark the quarter points on the new neckband and new neckline line, using straight pins or a fabric marker. Remember that, unless you have made the scoop of your neckline exactly the same on both the front and back, it is unlikely that the shoulder seams will be quarter points, so make sure you calculate these from the neckline measurement as a whole.

Top Tip!

Use this calculation method when working with stretch fabrics that need to be tight to the body, to remove the stretch excess from your pattern.

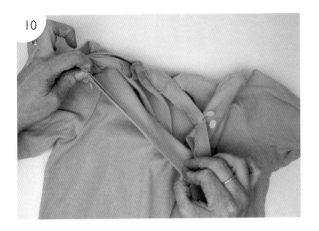

10. Match up the quarter points on the neckline and neckband. The neckband should be smaller than the neckline (see Top Tips). Pin or clip the neckband in place at these points.

11. Using an overlocker, or stretch stitch on your sewing machine, attach the neckband to the neckline edge, stretching the neckband to fit as you sew.

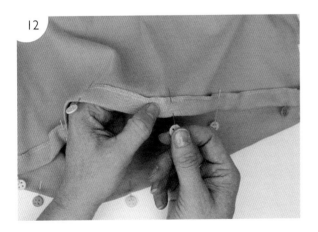

12. Fold up 2cm (¾") of hem along the bottom edge of the top, and pin or clip in place.

13. Attach a twin needle to your sewing machine, if you have one. If you haven't, one needle sewing two lines of parallel stitching will also work. Stitch along the hem edge from the front

side (if you are using a twin needle), securing the hem and recreating the look of the cover stitching that was there originally. Repeat the process around the neckline, catching down the overlocked seam to the body of the top. This will further help the neckband to lie flat.

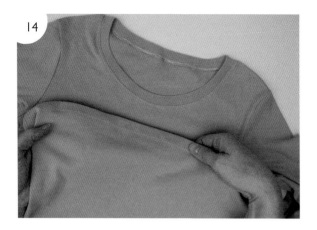

14. Give everything a good press with an iron to complete your new wider-necked top.

Top Tips

» If you don't want to lose any length from your top, why not create the new neckband from some jersey in a contrasting colour? It's a great way to use up scraps.

» Cutting the neckband smaller than the neckline, then stretching it to fit, allows the neckline to spring back and sit flush against the body, for a much neater, more professional finish.

» If you want to widen a neckline on a top that isn't made from a stretch fabric, consider using bias binding to edge the fabric, or to create a narrow facing along the new neckline.

PROJECT 15

EXPANDABLE TROUSER LEGS

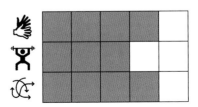

Skinny jeans and slim-leg trousers have been in fashion for a long time. However, they aren't always the most accommodating style. This project enables you to insert fabric panels down the sides of your trouser legs, which can be worn open or closed depending on your mood and access needs. This is great if you experience lymphodema of the legs, lower limb swelling, wear a catheter or a prosthetic, need to access your legs for medical treatments, find putting on tight trousers challenging, or if you simply want to change up the look of your trousers with a fun contrast panel, or switch the style from narrow leg to wide leg.

If dexterity around using zips is a challenge, why not use a chunky zip, or one with a ring style zipper pull to make it easier to use.

What you will need:

- A pair of trousers
- A stretch fabric of a similar weight to your trousers (I'm using stretch cotton twill)
- On-the-roll zipper to the length of your trouser legs
- Vlieseline T20 Edge Tape
- Iron and ironing board, or similar
- Stitch ripper or snips
- Straight pins
- Tape measure
- Fabric shears
- Sewing machine
- Hand sewing needle (optional)
- Needle threader (optional)
- Matching sewing thread
- Contrast thread for basting

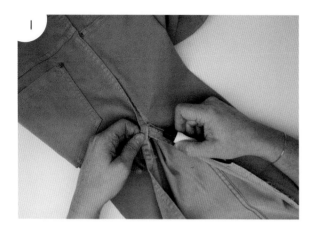

1. Unpick the outside leg seam using a stitch ripper or tool of your choice. In this example, the seam is a run and fell seam, which involves more unpicking than a straight seam. Unpick as high as you can, stopping short of any metalwork or rivets. Don't go all the way up to the waistband.

2. As my trousers are constructed using a run and fell seam, I have snipped into the seam allowance at the top of where I have opened the

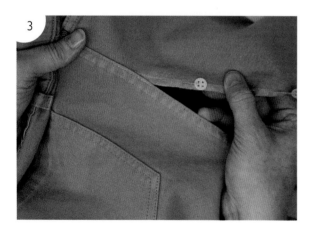

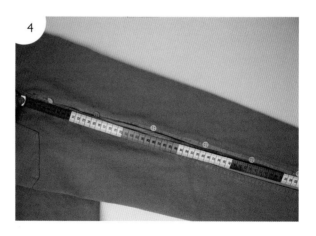

seam to help the seam fold back on itself. If your trousers are constructed with a straight seam, you can skip this step.

3. Pin the seam allowance back on both sides of the trouser leg to create neat edges. Top stitch the trouser seam where the two halves of the trousers cross, so that the seam is secure and sits flat.

4. Measure the length of the opening you have created down the side of your trouser leg. Add on a good amount of excess at both ends to allow for seam allowance and stretch. My trouser seam measures 75.5cm (30").

5

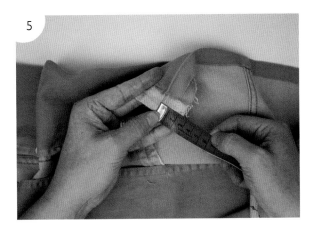

5

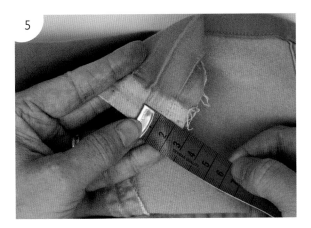

I added 6cm (2¼") to this measurement, making the full length 81.5cm (32¼").

5. The trousers should have a hem at the bottom. Unpick some of this hem so you can measure the fabric included in the hem. This measurement will need

to be added to your trouser length, otherwise the fabric panel being inserted will be too short. For my trousers, the hem is 2.5cm (1"). When this is added to the overall length calculated in step 4, the measurement is 84cm (33¼").

6

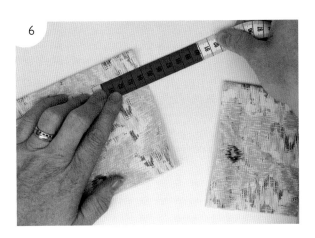

7

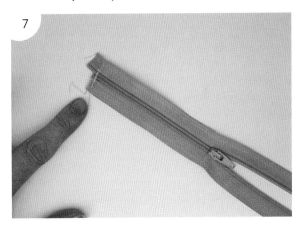

6. Cut a length of fabric to the width you would like your extension to be. Here, I have cut my fabric to 24cm (9½") wide to make a nice wide leg. Cut the strip of fabric to the length you calculated in step 5.

7. To accommodate the length of the zip required for this project, and to avoid unnecessary bulk at the thigh, I recommend using an on-the-roll zip. This may mean you need to attach the zipper pull, in which case do this now. Stitch across the end of the zip to stop the zipper pull sliding off the coil.

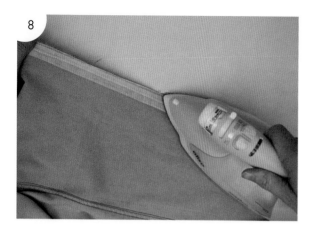

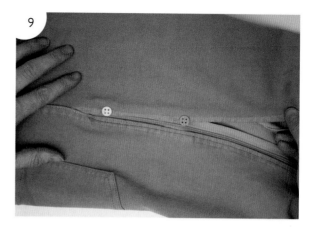

8. Remove the pins from the edges of your trouser leg and open out the fabric. Using your iron, apply some Vlieseline T20 Edge Tape along the full lengths of the seam edges, on the wrong side of the fabric. This tape will

prevent the seams from stretching out of shape as you stitch them.

9. Fold the seam edges back under and pin the zipper tape to both sides. Baste the zip in place using a long basting stitch on your sewing machine

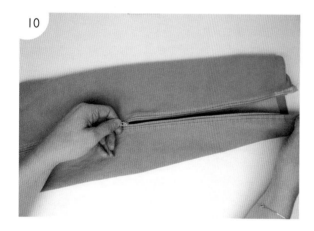

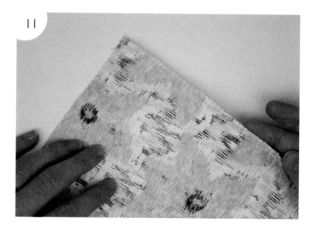

to hold it in position temporarily. Make sure you keep the top of the fabric as flat as possible to the zipper tape to avoid the seam bubbling at this point.

10. Once you have basted the zipper into place, try running the zipper pull up and down to check it moves smoothly.

11. Run an overlocking stitch, overcasting stitch or zigzag stitch around the outside of the fabric panel to prevent fraying. This is easier to do before inserting it into the trouser seam.

12. Pin one edge of the fabric panel under the zipper tape on one side of the trouser leg. The edge of the fabric

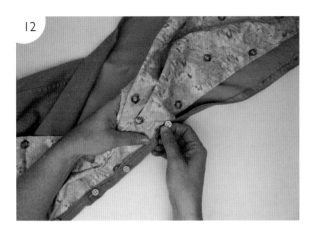

should line up with the edge of the tape. This can be fiddly so take your time. When positioning the fabric panel, make sure you leave some fabric at the top that sits higher than the opening (see step 14 to see why).

13. Top stitch two parallel lines of stitching (to replicate the look of the original run and fell seam) down the edge of the zip, catching in the trousers, zipper tape and fabric panel all together. This can be tricky at

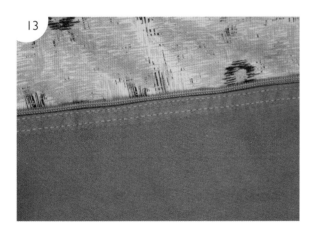

the top of the trouser seam, so work out what is most comfortable and manageable for you when doing this step. Remove the basting thread from this seam. Repeat this step on the other side of the trousers and fabric panel.

14. Once the panel is attached to the trousers down both sides of the trouser seams, turn the trouser leg inside out. At the top of the seam there will be an excess of fabric from the inserted panel. Fold this excess of fabric into a box pleat – so the opening of the fabric sits in the centre and the excess

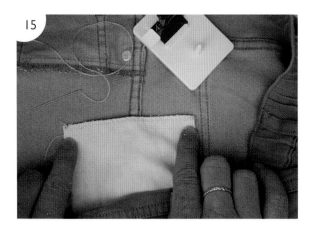

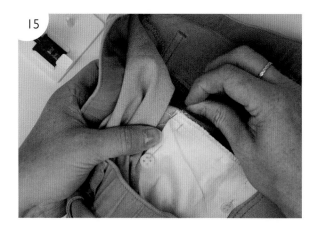

fabric sits flat to it. Pin this fabric and stitch along the top edge, holding it together.

15. Lay the trousers flat, and the box pleated panel end flat on top. Pin in place and secure in the corners using

a small hand stitch. If hand stitching isn't something you are able to do, this step can be done using a sewing machine, although this will mean the stitching will be more visible from the

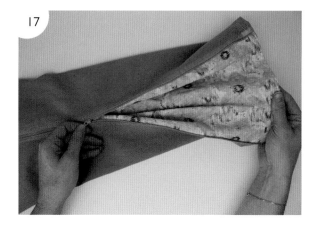

outside. Either way, the important thing is to catch the ends of the fabric flat so they don't fold or rub against the skin when the trousers are being worn.

16. The final step in making your expandable trousers is to neaten the hem. Turn up the fabric as it was

before you unpicked it, continuing with the added panel too, and top stitch in place.

17. Your expandable trouser leg is now complete. Test the zip to check it runs smoothly. Repeat these steps on the second leg of your trousers, if required.

Top Tips

» The wider the fabric for your inserted panel, the more bulk there will be against the leg when the zip is fastened. The same applies for the thickness of the fabric you use. Bear this in mind when deciding the width of the panel you insert.

» If dexterity around using zips is a challenge, why not use a chunky zip, or one with a ring style zipper pull to make it easier to use.

» When you baste on your sewing machine, use a contrast colour thread so the stitches are easy to see when you are removing them. However, avoid very light coloured thread on dark fabric, and very dark coloured thread on light fabric. This is because, when the basting threads are removed, they can leave filaments behind, which will show if the thread is a strong contrast.

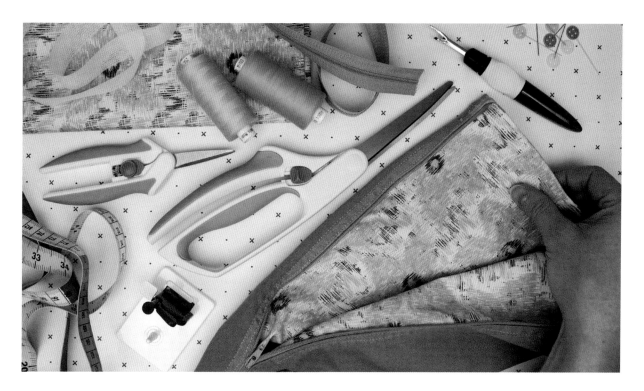

Kat Paylor Bent

Kat launched her company, Seated Sewing, in the North of England, inspired by her need to find clothes that worked for her when she became wheelchair-bound aged thirty, after a spinal injury resulted in cauda equina syndrome, which led to cervical spondylosis.

"Go for it! Just try it! You're not going to know if sewing is for you until you try. And, if you do, all of a sudden, the world of fashion opens up. And if it goes wrong, you always have your unpicker."

HOW DID YOU GET INTO SEWING?

I was brought up in a sewing family. My grandma was a seamstress and my mum sewed. As a child, there was always a sewing machine on the dining room table, so sewing was second nature to me. It was just something we did. We would never buy clothes; they were always made for us and, as a 5' 11" tall woman growing up in the 80s, this was a godsend. Back then, there were no tall ranges so I could never find what I needed in the shops, even before I became disabled. However, as I knew from an early age how to sew, I was able to use my skills to make myself trousers that fitted. When I was made disabled, I realised that none of the clothes I had in my wardrobe fitted me properly anymore. My newly disabled body was different to the way it had been before and the clothes I once loved to wear no longer worked. I was in bed for the first nine months and this changed my body shape. Not only did my clothing no longer fit, it was also very uncomfortable. This was exacerbated when I was fitted with a colostomy bag and catheter. I could no longer tolerate anything around my waist. The position where waistbands would sit on my body became a real stumbling block to being able to wear the clothes I wanted to wear.

Sewing actually became a part of my rehabilitation. As I was bed-bound a fair amount in the early years, I started to sew again, concentrating on what I could make from bed. This was mostly things like embroidery cards as they were nice and small, and it helped me adjust to concentrating on patterns and doing hand sewing. I was still on a lot of drugs at this point, so the cards were easy projects to pick up when I was able to and put down when I wasn't.

I followed these with small hand sewn projects, such as quilting small cushions and pillowcases. As my sewing ability progressed with my recovery, we were able to set up my sewing machine on a small table that moved over the bed, and I controlled it with buttons. Initially, I focused on doing minor alterations and adaptations until I'd regained the strength to move from the bed to a specialist chair, which meant I was able to access the foot pedal again.

WHAT CHALLENGES HAVE YOU FACED WITH ACCESSING THE CRAFT?

I initially found sourcing suitable fabrics a real challenge. Trying to find fabrics that were comfortable to wear, but also breathable for sitting on a plastic wheelchair seat all day, proved a steep learning curve. There were no commercial patterns available either so I had to really teach myself how to create and adapt my own sewing patterns.

Another challenge was finding sewing equipment designed with disabled people in mind. In the early days, I had to hack and adapt all my sewing kit. There is far more available now but back then it was a real struggle. It could still be better but at least things are starting to move in the right direction. One example of this was when I resorted to raiding my son's school pencil case. My cervical spondylosis means my vertebrae are crumbling, which puts pressure on my discs and spinal column. This can result in my losing the ability to grip with my hands. When my hands are having a bad day, I find it challenging to hold on to things, so I started using one of my son's rubber pencil grips on my chalk pencils to help me hold them.

Something else I use that has definitely helped me is my retractable tape measure. This works brilliantly for me because the tape reels itself away and I don't have to worry about it trailing on the floor and getting caught in my wheels. I also use homemade pattern weights. I find the ones you can buy from haberdashers just aren't heavy enough, so I use heavy washers that we found in a DIY store. These are weighty enough to hold my pattern pieces in place so they don't slip.

WHAT CHALLENGES DO YOU HAVE WITH CLOTHING?

As I've mentioned, after becoming disabled, the realisation that none of the clothes I used to wear fit me anymore was a bit of a shock. There was a point when I realised I really missed my old clothes. Before I became disabled, I worked in high-level management and

MEET THE MAKER

used to sit on a Board. I really enjoyed wearing good quality, smart clothing every day in my job, and I missed that part of my identity. When I looked on the high street and online, I just couldn't find anything that made me feel special the way those outfits did that would also work for a being in a wheelchair. There was either a lot of material in the backs of the garments, making them bulky and uncomfortable for wearing seated, or the trousers weren't long enough, or the skirts would sit incorrectly on my body. Waistbands with no give in them also made these garments totally impractical for me. This was the inspiration I needed and I decided to go back to what I knew: I would create my own clothing that worked for me and my needs. I did a lot of pattern hacking, adapting sewing patterns to accommodate what I needed from clothing. And that's where the incentive came from to start Seated Sewing. When others saw what I was doing, they would ask me to make them outfits too. I was finally able to create clothing that felt comfortable and useable, but was also stylish and fashionable.

ANY TIPS OR ADVICE?

I have learned that creating a sewing space is really important for sewing to be accessible for me – this is one of the main pieces of advice I would give to a fellow sewer. My sewing space is set up in an L-shaped formation, with two work tables: one is for my sewing machine and the other for my overlocker. I position my wheelchair between the two so I can access them both easily. My overlocker table doubles up as a cutting table for when I'm cutting out my fabric pieces. Everything is raised to the height that works with my wheelchair, which is really important. I have a dress form I use, mainly for draping fabric, and I've adjusted the height of that too so it's workable for me. I don't want to have to stretch out for anything as this can cause strain and stress on my body, so it's important that everything is within arm's reach. If I need to use the dress form for longer skirts, for example, I will just raise it up so that it's at the right height for that project. I use an adjustable dress form as this allows me to make it fit my proportions. If there's an adjustable version of something, that's the one I'm choosing!

I don't really have a set place for everything in my sewing space – I'm usually pretty good at knowing if something is missing, or not where it should be. However, I do fully recommend having a sewing caddy or box next to your machine with everything in it you need. That way you aren't searching around for things when you want them and everything is within easy reach.

One of the most important investments you'll make on your sewing journey is your sewing machine. This is doubly important when it comes to access needs. I use a machine with a knee lift, which is great because I'm able to use my legs and the knee lift frees up my hands to sew. If you're a wheelchair user without use of your legs, then a machine with a stop-start button is a must. This enables you to use your machine without the need for a foot pedal. For ease, I use a machine with an automatic needle threader and thread cutter. It makes everything easier and quicker and I would never choose a machine that didn't have these options now. Advancements in technology can help too. I have all my sewing machines linked to my smart speakers so I can just ask for them to be turned on or off and it happens automatically. This saves me having to reach round and turn them all off individually.

I use a standard ironing board for my pressing work and an Oliso iron that lifts automatically when you release the handle. This has been a great addition to my sewing space as I don't need to lift the iron up and down manually, which saves my wrists and arms. I also have a small, half-size ironing board I can use if I'm unable to use my full-size ironing board. If I'm only working on very small projects and just need to iron small sections, I'll use a sleeve arm and a very small mini craft iron – a bit like a soldering iron but with a flat ironing attachment.

One machine I absolutely love and use all the time is my coverstitch machine. I appreciate this isn't a usual addition to a sewing room but I invested in one and it's great for helping me make clothing that works for me. Being a wheelchair user, I find that if garments have bulky seams at the back, these can be very uncomfortable to sit on. I construct all my back trouser seams as if they are for leggings, using my coverstitch machine. This means the seams are flat and don't rub when I am sitting against them.

With regard to choosing fabrics, again, as a wheelchair user, I always choose natural fabrics. Synthetic fabrics tend to be more slippery and they aren't breathable, which clothes need to be when you're sitting on a plastic wheelchair seat all day. I shop for

Kat's Top Tips

1. Make sure everything in your sewing space is accessible and that you can move around the area easily with minimal effort.

2. Adjust the heights of your tables and dress forms so you can sit comfortably at them. This avoids putting strain on your body.

3. Use a sewing machine with as many automatic features as possible. I recommend a knee lift, stop-start button, automatic thread cutter and needle threader.

4. Link up your sewing machines to your smart speaker to make turning them on and off automatic and easy.

5. Keep all your sewing kit in a caddy near your sewing machine so you don't have to move around to search for things.

my fabrics online a lot, so the fabric descriptions are really important to me. I only shop from places that have really clear, accurate descriptions of the fabrics they are selling, as this helps me make informed choices.

I love to use linens and cotton lawns. These are beautiful to work with and comfortable to wear. If a fabric is going to be near the skin, I prefer to use bamboo, especially bamboo jersey. Bamboo is a great option, in particular if you have a colostomy or catheter, as it has natural antibacterial properties; very

important for keeping your skin clean and healthy.

The fabrics I tend to avoid are polyesters, lycra, and anything with elastane in it, as these fabrics are not at all breathable and leave me feeling sweaty and uncomfortable. I absolutely love to work with crepe de chine or satin back crepe, but these are really slippery fabrics so I would never use them to make trousers or skirts – I'd slip straight out of my chair! However, I would use them to make a top if the garment called for something with a level of luxury and drape.

Meet the Maker
Favourite Tools

1. **HEAVY PATTERN WEIGHTS**

2. **RUBBER PENCIL GRIPS**

3. **RETRACTABLE TAPE MEASURE**

Kat Paylor Bent

You can find Kat on IG @seatedsewing
FB @seatedsewinguk & www.seatedsewing.co.uk

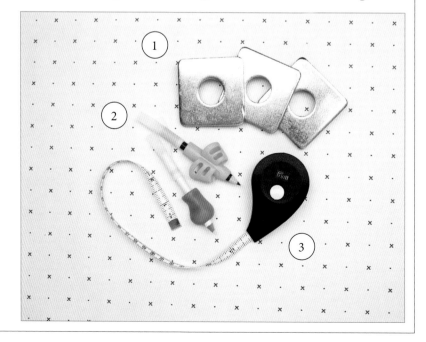

Conclusion

You've made it – thank you! It's been wonderful to take this journey with you and I hope you've enjoyed reading it as much as I have writing and compiling it.

We need to talk about disability and accessibility. Disability isn't a bad word! The more we talk about our differences, the better the world will become, in my opinion. Sewing is one small piece of that world but what an important piece it is. Fabric is part of our everyday life and whatever genre you choose to work in, be it dressmaking, quilting, bag making, soft furnishings, or alterations and adjustments as this book focuses on, just know that everyone can sew with the right tools and accommodations.

Clothing has always been hugely important to identity, as far back as history is recorded. Wealth, social standing, position, culture, personality and environment all come together to inform how we dress our bodies. When we don't have access to clothing that serves us, it can affect every area of our lives – our wellbeing, our ability to exist in our environment, to do our job and to express ourselves. This has been the reality for the disabled community forever. Our needs have never been put first. Thankfully, now, the conversations are starting to be had, and my hope is that this book can be a part of those conversations.

If, having read this book, you've felt inspired to start sewing, to pick it up again after a long absence, to start creating your own accessible wardrobe, to make something for your loved ones, or even to start a business offering a service to the disabled community, then I am over the moon and have achieved everything I wanted to with it: to inspire and empower through the medium of sewing. I hope this will be the first of many books, and the initial step on a really exciting journey of All Access Sewing. Who knows where this will take us all!

I have learned a huge amount in writing this book and have met some incredible people. All the inspiring voices within these pages have gifted us so much amazing advice and guidance; if you relate to any of them, please follow them on the socials. The consistent message throughout, however, from everyone involved, has been: just go for it; give it a go. You have nothing to lose by taking those first steps and there is always a way to make something work. Mistakes can be unpicked, lessons will be learned and your learning curve will probably be steep! But just try it – then be kind to yourself, have patience as you grow, and embrace whatever part of sewing brings you joy.

Please come and join the conversation and be a part of the All Access Sewciety Facebook group, where we share tips, advice and support in a friendly, inclusive and accessible space.

And do check out www.allaccesssewing.com where you'll find lots of information, blog posts, and an accessibility store full of everything you'll need to kit out yourself and your sewing space.

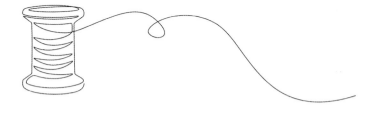

About the Author

Rebecca (or Becky as she is affectionately known) doesn't remember a time when sewing wasn't part of her life. She jokes that she was born with a needle in her hand. Her first sewing machine was her grandmother's old hand-wound Jones machine, at which she would spend hours sewing beautiful creations for her teddies and dolls. These creations no doubt fell apart as soon as they were finished, but the seed of joy at creating with fabric was "sewn" and a life path forged.

University was where Rebecca really grew into her craft. An intense passion for corsetry drew her to seek a formal education, studying at the London College of Fashion, where she learned how to design and cut period patterns for costume.

In the early 2000s, the BBC offered an apprenticeship scheme called "Vision". Graduating at the top of her class, Rebecca was one of a small handful of graduates who was offered a work place with the BBC in a costume department.

Rebecca loved her work in the television industry and has since worked in live television, demonstrating sewing machines for Create & Craft TV. She was also Assistant Sewing Producer on Series 8 of *The Great British Sewing Bee*, and was invited to join the production team for a brand-new Channel 4 docu-series, *Unique Boutique*, a show in which fashion and clothing are adapted to suit the bodies of people from all walks of life.

Rebecca is late-diagnosed autistic and ADHD. She and her husband, Stuart, have two daughters, Imogen and Amelia.

Becky Cole

Becky is a professional sewer and pattern cutter, having sewn since early childhood. She is late-diagnosed autistic and ADHD and has Irlen Syndrome. Learning that she has lived with three separate disabilities has had an enormous impact on her sewing journey, not least giving her the inspiration to write this book!

"If you are intrigued by sewing, my guess is you will love sewing. It may take you a while to find your genre or technique, but that's ok. It isn't a race to try to win. But until you try, you'll never know!"

HOW DID YOU GET INTO SEWING?

I've been sewing since I was seven years old. I don't know what it was that drew me to it or made me choose it as a hobby, but the minute I started to use my grandmother's old sewing machine to make things from scraps of fabric, I was hooked. I grew up as an undiagnosed autistic and ADHD child and, as such, I found the world around me confusing and never really felt as though I fitted into it. No matter what I did, I always felt I was existing on the periphery while everyone around me was fully engaged. I struggled with friendships and social communication, and sewing became a refuge for me. I could lose myself for days in projects and the world made sense. I also discovered that, when I made clothing for myself, people were always interested, fascinated by my process and impressed by my young skills. Conversation felt easy when I was showing off my latest make. Sewing just became the thing I did that grew from a hobby, to a passion, to a career.

WHAT CHALLENGES HAVE YOU FACED WITH ACCESSING THE CRAFT?

Autism and ADHD are two conflicting neuro conditions. For me, I find that one thrives on routine, detail, and methodical repetition and perfectionism. The other prefers novelty, instant gratification, and is thoroughly disinterested in repetition. I discovered I was neurodivergent aged thirty-nine, so most of my sewing experience was developed without knowing this about myself. As is a common theme amongst the late diagnosed, I'd just decided I was lazy, or useless, and could never care enough about the finishing details to class myself as good as those I saw around me. So, I always tried harder and harder. Now I understand myself better, I have far more patience with myself when I'm sewing. I now realise why I've always swayed towards dressmaking rather than other genres of sewing. The repetitive nature of cutting and sewing that's involved in quilt making appeals to my autistic side but the ADHD part of my brain gets very disinterested very quickly at the lack of novelty. Soft furnishings don't challenge me enough (too many straight lines) and I don't make bags because my autistic brain likes the familiarity of only using one bag all the time. I only change my bag if the one I'm currently using has fallen apart! Making clothes appeals to the novelty my brain craves, while dressmaking patterns and pattern drafting appeal to my need for familiarity, structure and rules.

"I use an overlocker all the time, especially because I make a lot of things from jersey and an overlocker is the best way to sew up stretch garments, in my opinion."

WHAT CHALLENGES DO YOU HAVE WITH CLOTHING?

One of the first things I did when I learned I was neurodivergent was pull my wardrobe apart. I always wore clothing that I thought I was supposed to wear. Then on days when I was at home, I would live in leggings and a hoody and be blissfully happy. Once the Pandora's box of sensory awareness was open, I found I could tolerate uncomfortable clothing and materials less and less. I find clothes shopping overwhelming: too many people, bright lights and too much noise. If I don't find what I'm looking for immediately, I get very frustrated. Changing rooms are horrific environments for me but I MUST try on to find whether a garment is a sensory yes or no. I can order online or take things home to try on, but the reality of my ADHD brain is that I will inevitably forget to return items within the returns timeframe and end up stuck with clothes I don't want or need.

My wardrobe is also very monotone (I adore an autumnal palette!) with little pattern. Where many people find colour brings them joy, I've always kept to a drab, monochrome colour scheme. Since being diagnosed with

Irlen Syndrome, I've realised that my choice of colour and plain fabrics has been because my brain can't process contrast. It actually causes me pain to wear bright colours and patterns so, once again, I'm just allowing my wardrobe to be what I want it to be, with zero judgement.

I've learned that, once I find an item of clothing that is "safe", I will buy it in several different colours so I can wear it all the time, with the illusion that I'm dressing differently each day. Part of deciding to make my own clothes was to try to bypass the need to navigate shops for clothing. However, I've lost count of the number of times I would be so excited to make myself a garment, then hate it the minute I tried it on. Because you can't "try before you make" with dressmaking, I was put off making clothes for myself for a long time as I found it soul destroying. My favourite thing to do now is to take garments I already own that I love to wear, take a pattern from them and remake them in different fabrics and colours.

ANY TIPS OR ADVICE?

My sewing room exists in two states: either show-home-level organised or tornado chic. My neurodivergent brain can't cope with chaos and thrives in a clean and tidy environment. However, it also means I'm incapable of controlling the chaos. I've learned ways of organising my sewing space with this in mind. First, I forgive myself when things get out of hand. I've changed the inner commentary from "lazy and useless" to "living with a disability – I can only do what I can do". I'm lucky enough to have a room in my house I can use as a sewing room. I appreciate not everyone will have this privilege. However, having a closed-off space where I don't need to clear up at the end of the day, and can shut the door on the chaos, does help my mindset amazingly. If you have a space you can dedicate to your craft that can be hidden by a door/curtain/tablecloth, this can help with the "busy brain bees" a lot.

I try to organise my space so that everything has a home. It doesn't always work and if I have something that doesn't have a specific place to live, it will be relegated to one of the many DOOM piles (Didn't Organise, Only Moved) in my sewing space. If something has a specific home I will try to make sure it goes back where it needs to be. I also experience object impermanence, which means if I put something down, I instantly lose it. I tried using a lanyard with my snips on to avoid this but I kept forgetting to put it on.

The key to supporting my neurodivergent brain is to make things as easy as possible to reduce the amount of executive function required to follow through with a task; even one as simple as putting my scissors away. Sewing is my job, and thus my sewing room is my office. I spend a lot of time in there and can use many "spoons" working at my sewing machine. At the end of the work day, I can only use the "spoons" I have left to reorganise my space.

Another area I try to make as simple as possible is the steps involved in sewing. As mentioned, I used to think I was just lazy and didn't care about doing things properly or seeing them through to completion, but since discovering I'm ADHD, I've begun to understand that this is just my brain trying to maintain the novelty and therefore my own level of interest. For example, I've trained myself to sew without straight pins. I only pin when absolutely necessary. I never tack, although I will occasionally machine baste if I feel it'll make the next step easier. If I can sew it on a machine rather than sew by hand, then I will. (The day I learned how to sew a button on with my sewing machine was a very happy one!) I rarely (if ever) hand sew unless I absolutely have to. I adore cross stitch and hand embroidery, but these are separate crafts that I choose to do; I don't enjoy hand sewing when it's not my choice. I've found thousands of little ways to streamline my sewing practice, which means I can now sew very quickly using as little mental energy as possible.

I use a sewing machine with a built-in needle threader and a knee lift because it streamlines my sewing experience. I also love a thread cutter on the machine because as soon as I put down my snips, I instantly lose them (object impermanence). Lastly, a machine with a bobbin and top thread alarm is an absolute must. This is an alert on your machine that notifies you that your bobbin thread has run out or your top thread has snapped. Such an advance in technology has been like an answer to my childhood prayers and now I can't be without it. ADHD is literally defined by an inability to effectively direct one's attention – spotting that a bobbin has run out has never been my strong point!

I use an overlocker all the time, especially because I make a lot of things from jersey and an overlocker is the best way to sew up stretch garments, in my opinion. However, I don't own an air threader and have to thread up my overlocker manually. Although I can do this, it's a fiddle and, if my executive function is low, it can feel so overwhelming I will just stop what I'm doing and never come back to it. I'm not ashamed to say that, if I'm making a garment for myself, I will just use the same colour for all my overlocking rather than rethread it! When I was much younger, I bought an ex-display overlocker from a shop, which was threaded up with yellow thread. For years I just overlocked everything in yellow, calling it my "trademark". I didn't know I was ADHD back then, but it's one of the things that makes sense now.

My sewing kit is made up of items that bring me joy. I have items from grandmothers' sewing boxes; I have

"I try to organise my space so that everything has a home."

items that hold a lot of happy memories for me; and I have items that feel nice to hold and use. I prefer a heavier, longer pair of fabric shears because I love the way they feel in my hand, and the sound of a sharp blade slicing through fabric at the start of a project is one that fills my every cell with joy. Again, any items that make life easier or create a shorter route to the end goal are winning tools for me. I love fabric pens that erase with heat, because they're easy to use and the marks are simple to remove. Ironing rulers are great too because they can make pressing up a seam allowance much easier. Another tool I only discovered relatively recently is loop turners – a game changer for anyone who finds sitting and concentrating on a fiddly task like turning through fabric loops hard to do.

One of my favourites is actually something I came across while researching this book. I now wouldn't be without my Zirkel pin magnet. This is a metal dish with a strong magnet, which automatically arranges your pins in a circle with the heads facing outwards. I have no idea how it works but it has revolutionised my sewing organisation! I always have copious amounts of straight pins because I lose them so quickly and need a constant supply. With my Zirkel, I can just throw my pins in the general direction of the dish and they will land where I need them to. Because the heads are facing outwards, too, it means they are far easier to grab when needed. No rummaging around in pin

pots. Plus, the novelty appeals to my eternal search for dopamine so, for me, it's a win-win!

When it comes to fabric, I've learned I must feel it before I buy it. The fabrics I wear against my skin play a huge part in my creating a sensory friendly wardrobe, so I can't just buy a fabric blind. I will often get a favourite fabric in multiple colours so I have a stock of "safe" fabrics in my stash. I absolutely adore

Becky's Top Tips

1. Create a sewing space that can be covered over or shut away when you're not using it, so any pressure to clear away is removed.

2. Try to allocate a place for everything. This makes it easier to control the chaos and to find the items you've misplaced.

3. Give yourself permission to skip the unimportant steps. It's ok to streamline your process.

4. Choose a sewing machine with a bobbin alarm to alert you when your bobbin is running low.

5. Always feel your fabrics before choosing to make a garment from them, and wash them to make sure you can still tolerate the feel of them post-washing.

anything with a stretch to it. Lightweight jerseys are my favourite. I also love stretch denim (I mean LOTS of stretch), and anything that will move with my body. Natural fibres, such as cotton and bamboo, are best against my skin (feeling sweaty is a big sensory "no" for me, as is generally feeling too hot), but I also love fabrics such as viscose and lyocell. If a fabric doesn't have a stretch to it, I'll make the garment a couple of sizes too big and add elastic to the waist to allow it to move with me.

I always advise people to wash their fabric before using it. This is called pre-shrinking and is very important whatever your situation. It means that any natural shrinkage in the fabric occurs BEFORE you cut out your pattern pieces, avoiding your perfectly fitting garment shrinking on its first wash. From a sensory point of view, washing a fabric causes any starches or dressings on the fabric to be removed, which can, in turn, change how a fabric feels, either for better or worse. This means I can thoroughly assess how a fabric will feel to wear before committing my time to making a full garment from it.

Meet the Maker

Favourite Tools

1. ZIRKEL PIN MAGNET DISH

2. HEAVY FABRIC SHEARS

3. LOOP TURNERS

Becky Cole

You can find Becky on IG @becky_cole_sensory_sewer
FB @becky cole sensory sewer & www.allaccesssewing.com

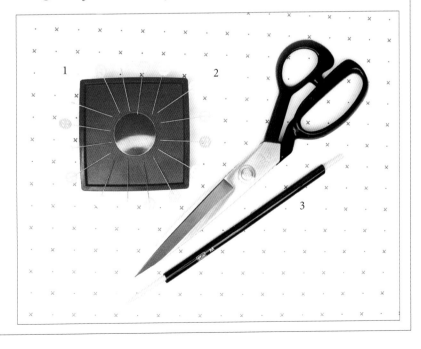

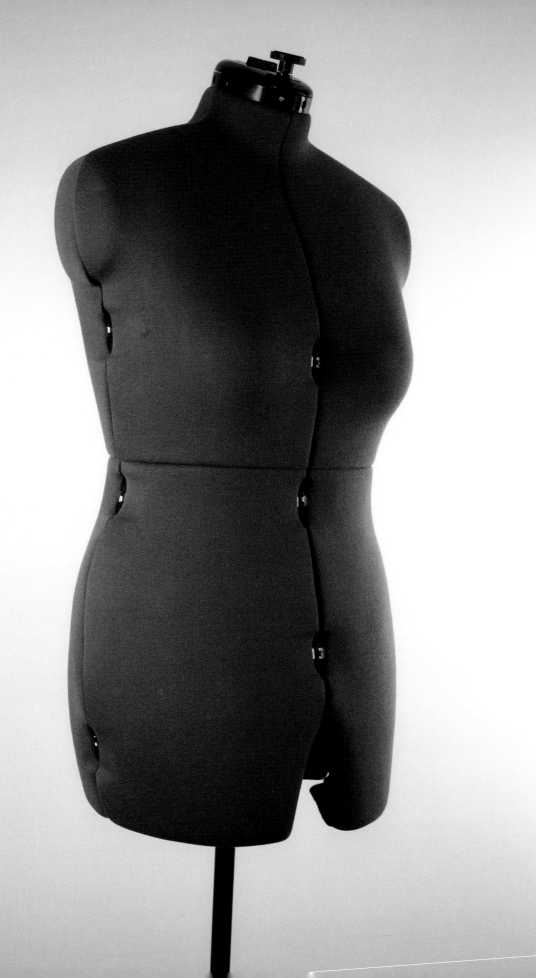

Acknowledgements

First, I would like to take a moment to thank you, the reader, for choosing my book and deciding to be a part of this conversation. I have always dreamed of writing a book and I believe I can only call myself an author because you have picked up my book and made it a part of your world.

The biggest thank you goes to my husband, Stu. Stu has been by my side since we were children; we have grown up together. He has supported me through every stage of my life and every grand idea I have ever had. Throughout the ups and downs, he has been my steady hand, my rock – especially over the last couple of years since I've realised I am autistic and ADHD. Witnessing someone you love unpack their entire life and adjust to a new identity, along with all the unmasking that can look from the outside like becoming a whole new person, can be tough. But Stu has stood by me and given me the love and space to grow into the person I am today. When I decided I wanted to write this book, he was there holding me up as he always has done. I wouldn't want to do any of this without him by my side.

My beautiful girls, Imogen and Milly, who inspire me every day, are the real reason this book has come into being. As a very neurodivergent household, the three of us can find life incredibly challenging. My sole reason for breathing is to make sure they know they are loved, and to try to make the world a better place for them to grow up in. As an undiagnosed neurodivergent child growing up in the 80s and 90s, the world back then was a place I just didn't fit into. I will not accept that for my girls, and I will fight to make it better. If nothing else, they make me want to realise my dreams so I can show them that, whatever they set their minds to, they too can make their lives what they want them to be.

To my mum and dad, Annette and Mike, who have always supported me and given me all the love a child could want – thank you for always helping me when I wanted to make something happen and for literally providing me with the means to make this book exist in the world! And thank you for always making me feel unconditionally loved, while the world made me feel broken.

Special thanks to Mary, my mother-in-law, for being both my biggest cheerleader and as excited to discuss a sewing project as I am!

To Alexa Whitten at The Book Refinery – thank you for seeing the vision and sharing my passion for this project when so many others didn't! And for answering my millions of questions: your matter-of-fact manner and awesome skill in making this book look so beautiful have been wonderful. And thanks to my amazing editor, Alexa Tewkesbury, for applying your incredible eye over my waffle and turning it into a book that is beautiful to read.

A huge thank you to Victoria Jenkins for writing my Foreword while trying to plan yet another London Fashion Week show – and basically take over the world, one accessible fashion statement at a time; for going from colleague to being a wonderful friend and cheerleader in the space of a few moments, and for being the voice of the movement we all need. This book definitely wouldn't exist if it wasn't for your encouragement and support, so thank you from the bottom of my heart.

To Yvonne Coleclough, Alycia Hirani, Kat Paylor Bent and Amber Brown for giving me your time and sharing your stories with me; for helping to inspire everyone reading this book with the confidence to believe that they too can pick up a needle and start to sew. You all encourage me enormously and it has been an honour to be a conduit for your stories.

Thank you to Stuart Hillard, Carrie Smith, Nigel May, Paula Milner, Paula Pascual, Triple Minor and Carla Bagshaw for writing me such wonderful testimonials. I was truly humbled by your words, kindness and support.

To Abigail Moore of Spud Digital for creating me a website under such a tight deadline and trying to work with my completely digital-phobic brain! You are a true professional and your patience knows no bounds. I look forward to taking the *All Access Sewing* brand to the next stage with you.

To my greatest friends and biggest supporters, Emily Crabtree, Michelle Hydes and Louise Murphy-Mohr, who, when all the self-doubt and negative inner talk kicked in, were always on the other end of the phone to dispel them and give me the boost of confidence I desperately needed. And for always seeing the best in me when I can't see it myself, and reminding me I am loved.

My family, Nicola, Sarah, John, and everyone who has wished me well and supported me from the sidelines. I love you all dearly.

I would like to thank Guy Baker at Brother, Andrew Groves at Groves, and Chris Clifton at Adjustoform for being so supportive of the project and for supplying imagery and equipment for the book.

Thank you to Thomas Davies of Thomas Byron Photography for taking my beautiful headshots and adapting them for this book.

I reserve a huge amount of gratitude for all the people out there working tirelessly to achieve true inclusion and accessibility for the disabled and neurodivergent communities, both within fashion and crafting, and all areas of life. It's people like you who make all the difference. Keep fighting the good fight.

And one final thank you to Liz Hunt, my art and textiles teacher. You created the only space at school where my undiagnosed neurodivergent self felt safe and happy, and you recognised my passion for sewing and nurtured it. I wouldn't be here doing any of this if it wasn't for you.

GLOSSARY

Adjustable piping foot

A sewing machine presser foot with a screw slider, used for making and attaching piping.

Air threader

A type of overlocker, or serger, where the threads are fed through the machine using puffs of air through channels, avoiding the necessity for manual threading.

Alteration

A change in an item of clothing's structure to better suit the needs of the wearer.

Automatic needle threader

An automation on a sewing machine that means the needle is threaded automatically by the machine rather than the user having to thread it manually.

Bar tack

A wide satin stitch created to form the ends of a buttonhole.

Baste

Another term for "tack", this means to stitch together temporarily using long stitches that are easy to remove.

Basting stitch

A long machine or hand stitch used to temporarily join fabric together.

Bespoke garment

A one-off garment made to the wearer's specific measurements and body shape.

Bias binding

A type of tape formed with the fabric cut at 45 degrees to the straight grain, across the "bias" of the fabric. This gives the tape a slight stretch, making it suitable for edging curves – for example, around armholes or necklines.

Bobbin

The spool that sits in the base of a sewing machine, wound with thread, which it feeds out to loop with the top or upper thread when the sewing machine is in use.

Bobbin alarm

An alert that sounds on some sewing machines to make the sewer aware that the bobbin thread is about to run out and needs refilling.

Bodice block

A basic pattern shape used as the basis for creating dress-making patterns for garments worn on the top half of the body.

Boning

A stiff material, usually made from plastic or metal, traditionally inserted into fabric channels to create a very structured garment.

Box pleat

A type of pleat formed by folding fabric in equally from both sides to a central point.

Button applying foot

A type of sewing machine presser foot used to apply buttons.

Buttonhole foot

A type of sewing machine presser foot designed to sew buttonholes.

Chalk hem marker

A gadget attached to the stand of a dress form that puffs chalk out to create a line around the hem of a garment, enabling the even marking of a hem line.

Chalk pencil

A pencil containing a chalk-like lead used for temporarily transferring pattern markings etc onto fabric.

Channel

A fabric tube created within a garment, usually to allow the passing through of elastic, tape, cord or similar.

Chunky zip

A type of statement zip with thick plastic or metal teeth, usually used for coats or outer garments.

Closures

Different forms of fastenings used to close a garment.

Coil

The teeth that interlock along a zip.

Computerised sewing machine

A type of sewing machine that is controlled by computer technology within it.

Commercial patterns

A mass-produced pattern used to create a fabric project.

Cotton tape

A form of fabric tape made from cotton that rarely has any stretch in it.

Cotton twill tape

A form of heavier weight cotton tape with no stretch and a characteristic diagonal grain.

Couture

Types of high-end, one-off-designed garments, usually made by hand to specific specifications.

Cover stitch

A specialised stitch formed by two needles that create parallel lines of stitching, while underneath, the thread is looped between. This stitch is designed to cover the edge of a hem and usually used with stretch knit fabrics.

Cover stitch machine

A specialist type of sewing machine that produces a cover stitch – a type of stitch traditionally used to hem and construct jersey garments.

Cross stitch

A form of hand embroidery using embroidery threads to form small, cross-shaped stitches that create a design.

Curved ruler

A type of ruler with curved edges used in pattern drafting.

Cutting machine

A type of machine programmed to cut out shapes, using a mat and blade, in paper, fabric, vinyl and other materials.

GLOSSARY

Cutting mat
A large mat, usually made of rubber, designed to absorb a cutting blade and protect the surface beneath.

Cutting table
A large table, traditionally set at standing height, used for cutting out patterns and large pieces of fabric.

Darts
Traditionally a triangular or diamond shape stitched into fabric to help shape the flat fabric around the curves of the body.

Drafting table
A large table, traditionally set at standing height, used for drawing out dressmaking patterns.

Drape
How much a fabric hangs in loose folds.

Draping
A form of pattern drafting involving pinning fabric to a dress form.

Drawstring
A cord fed through a channel in fabric and pulled to cinch the fabric in.

Dress form
A 3D model of a human body used in dressmaking for draping or to pin fabric to.

Dressmaking
The genre of sewing involving the making of garments typically worn on the human body.

Dressmaking patterns
Paper patterns laid over fabric and cut out to determine the size and shape of the fabric pieces required to make a garment.

Duckbill scissors
A form of scissors where the lower blade forms a wide, flat D shape, used for trimming down seams.

Edge stitch
A line of top stitching sewn a few millimetres away from the edge of the fabric.

Elastic
A cord or tape woven with rubber that returns to its original shape when stretched, sewn into clothing to allow for stretch.

Embellishment
Added decorative details.

Embroidery
A form of surface decoration using different stitches to create a pattern or image.

Embroidery machine
A type of sewing machine that embroiders onto fabric.

Embroidery scissors
Small, sharp sewing scissors used for cutting threads or small details.

Erasable fabric marker
A form of fabric pen with non-permanent ink which is usually removed by rubbing, with water or with heat.

Eye

The hole at the tip of the needle for the thread to pass through.

Fabric basting glue

A type of temporary fabric glue which won't clog up sewing needles and can hold fabric and notions in place, instead of pins or basting stitches.

Fabric clips

Small, spring-loaded clips used to hold fabric edges together in the place of pins.

Fabric loops

Fabric strips stitched together to make tubes, turned through and pressed to form straps, handles, fastenings, waist or shoulder ties, eyelets etc.

Fabric pen/marker

A type of pen used for marking fabric.

Facing

A short lining piece used to finish fabric edges, such as necklines, armholes or other openings.

Fastenings

Notions used in garments to help them open and close, for example, zips, buttons, magnets, popper tape, ties, hook and eye, hook and loop tape etc.

Fat quarter

A piece of fabric traditionally cut for quilting projects, created by cutting a metre of fabric into quarters.

Female side (poppers)

The side of a popper that has the socket.

Fitting shell

Another name for a bodice block.

Fly zip

A zipper opening sandwiched between a placket and a facing, traditionally used on the front of trousers.

Foot pedal

The part of the machine controlled with the foot to manage the speed of the sewing machine.

Fraying

When unfinished fabric edges unravel and the woven threads start to separate.

French seams

A type of seam created by sewing the fabric wrong sides together, trimming down, then stitching right sides together so that the raw edges are enclosed within the seam.

Gathering stitches

Long stitches used to gather up the fabric by pulling the threads.

Haberdashery

Small items used in sewing such as elastic, zips, thread, buttons etc. Items other than fabric and equipment needed to make a garment.

Hand finish

Hand sewing used for the finishing elements of a project, for example, hand sewing a hem or hand sewing on buttons.

GLOSSARY

Heat erasable
Fabric marks that can be removed by applying heat.

Hook and loop tape
A form of fastening consisting of two sides of tape, one with tiny stiff plastic hooks and the other with tiny nylon loops that interlock with the hooks. Traditionally comes in stick-on and sew-in varieties.

Hooks and eyes
A form of fastening consisting of a small metal loop and a small metal hook. Both have small holes, or eyes, through which they can be stitched to fabric. The hook slips into the loop to close.

Imperial
Traditional units of measurement using inches, feet, yards etc.

Industrial sewing machine
A very powerful type of sewing machine set into a table, which delivers two kinds of stitches (straight and zigzag) and is used in factories and by professionals.

Inside leg seam
The seam that runs from the inner ankle to the groin.

Interfacing
A type of fabric that is applied to the wrong side of another fabric, most commonly with heat, to stabilise or strengthen the other fabric.

Invisible zip
A form of zip with a tight coil and discreet pull which, when sewn into a garment, is invisible from the outside when closed.

Invisible zipper foot
A form of sewing machine foot used to sew in invisible zips.

Ironing pad
A foldable, padded, heatproof fabric pad that can be laid out and used as a transportable ironing surface.

Ironing plate
The metal base of an iron that gets hot.

Ironing ruler
A type of heatproof ruler that can be used to measure hems and be ironed over.

Knee lift
An L-shaped metal lever, fixed to the front of a sewing machine and controlled by the knees to lift and lower the presser foot.

Knit fabrics
Fabrics created by knitting the fibres together, often to create a stretch finish.

Lacing
A form of fastening traditionally using cord or ribbon looped through eyelets and pulled tight to close.

Long arm quilting machine
A type of industrial sewing machine used for quilting large areas.

Loop turner

A tube with a smaller stick that runs through the centre, used to turn through fabric loops quickly and easily.

Machine baste

A form of basting stitch created using a long stitch on a sewing machine.

Magnetic buttons

Small magnets enclosed in a plastic-film coating used in clothing in place of buttons.

Male side (poppers)

The side of the popper, also known as the stud part, that fits into the socket on the female side.

Mechanical sewing machine

A traditional type of sewing machine run by an engine controlled by levers and gears, without any computerised input.

Mechanical table

A type of table with adjustable legs that can be lowered or lifted depending on requirements. This is sometimes controlled by hand and sometimes electronically.

Metric

Modern units of measurement using millimetres, centimetres, metres etc.

Narrow roll hem

A fine hem created by a tight, narrow satin stitch along the edge of the fabric.

Needle puller

A gadget that clamps on to a needle or pins to assist in pulling them through fabric.

Needle threader

A gadget used to assist in the threading of needles.

Notch cutter

A gadget, looking similar to pliers, that cuts small snips into the edge of fabric to mark alignment points.

Notches

Small cuts in the edges of fabric pieces to create alignment points.

Notions

Small sewing items required for a project, such as buttons, zips, thread etc.

Off-the-peg

Clothing bought from shops that is mass-produced to set sizes.

On-the-roll zipper

A form of zip that comes in one long continuous roll and is cut to size, often with multiple pulls supplied.

Overcasting stitch

A form of sewing stitch that wraps around the edge of fabric to prevent fraying.

Overlocked seam

A seam finished using an overlocker.

GLOSSARY

Overlocker
A type of sewing machine that is used to finish seam edges or sew up stretch knit garments. A blade cuts the edge of the fabric while the three or four threads wrap the fabric edge to prevent fraying.

Oversew
To reinforce stitching by sewing a line of stitching repeatedly.

Patch pockets
A type of pocket that is applied on top of the fabric and top stitched in place.

Pattern
Cut-out paper shapes used to dictate the fabric shapes required to make up a garment, quilt or bag etc.

Pattern cutting
Creating dressmaking patterns.

Pattern drafting
Creating dressmaking patterns.

Pattern hacking
Adjusting and adapting paper patterns by cutting and sticking to change the shape and/or sizing.

Pattern pieces
The individual paper pattern shapes that are cut out from the pattern and applied to fabric ready for cutting.

Pattern weights
Heavy weights used in place of pins to hold pattern pieces in position ready for cutting. For use with a mat and rotary cutter.

PDF pattern
A form of digital sewing pattern that is printed off and stuck together before being cut out.

Peg board
A wall-mounted board covered in holes into which pegs are inserted. Used to store and hang tools and equipment.

Pinking
A zigzag form of edge cutting used to prevent fraying.

Pivot
The action of stopping sewing on a sewing machine, with the needle lowered into the fabric, and rotating the fabric at this point.

Placket
A strip of fabric that traditionally sits behind a fastening.

Plate
The metal base of a sewing machine underneath the presser foot.

Pliers
A tool formed of two spring-loaded handles and a metal tip, used for gripping and pulling.

Pocket bag
The fabric part of the pocket inside the opening.

Popper
A type of fastening, traditionally made from plastic or metal, where a male (or stud) piece snaps into a female (or socket) piece.

Popper tape

A fabric tape with poppers inserted along it.

Pre-shrink

The process of washing fabric, prior to cutting out pattern pieces, to remove any dressings and allow for natural shrinkage, avoiding this occurring after a garment is made.

Presser foot

The part of a sewing machine which lowers to clamp on to fabric while it is fed through the machine. The presser foot is usually interchangeable and can be switched to suit different tasks.

Pressing

The process of ironing fabric. Traditionally, pressing was the term to describe holding an iron on fabric, using the heat and weight of the iron to smooth it, rather than pushing the iron across the fabric.

Princess seam

A type of curved seam that traditionally runs from the armhole, over a bust point to the waist of a bodice.

Quilt making

The process of making quilts.

Quilting

Lines of top stitching sewn across the top of a quilt, through patchwork, wadding, and backing fabric layers, to hold the layers together and produce padded areas of texture.

Quilting cotton

A type of cotton fabric designed for use in quilt making.

Rouleaux loop

A very fine fabric loop used to create button or lacing loops.

Ribbing

Narrow bands of stretch fabric traditionally used to create cuffs and hems on sweatshirts.

Right side

The side of the fabric that is on show on a finished project.

Ring pull

A hoop-shaped zipper pull.

Rivets

Small metal embellishments added to areas of clothing to increase strength, such as corners of pockets on jeans.

Roll hem

A type of hem created by turning up a small amount of fabric, then turning it up again and stitching it in place.

Rotary cutter

A fabric-cutting implement that uses a retractable blade rolled along the edge of the fabric to cut it.

Ruler handle

A handle, applied with plastic suckers to plastic sewing rulers, to allow easy manoeuvring of the ruler.

GLOSSARY

Run and fell seams

A type of high-strength seam traditionally found on jeans and work trousers. The seam is stitched together, one side trimmed down, and the other side rolled over and top stitched down, encasing the raw edges.

Satin stitch

A stitch formed with a zigzag stitch set to a very short stitch length, creating a wide line of close stitches.

Seam

The line where two pieces of fabric are stitched together.

Seam allowance

The amount of fabric between the edge of the fabric and the seam line.

Serger seams

The American term for overlocked seams.

Sewing caddy

A box or container in which a sewing kit is stored.

Sewing kit

A collection of tools and equipment that enables a person to sew.

Sewing pattern

A paper document with shapes marked on it designed to be cut out and used as templates for cutting out fabric, so as to create the correct shapes to make a garment, bag or similar.

Shears

Long, sharp scissors designed for cutting through layers of fabric.

Side seam

A seam that runs down the sides of a garment.

Sleeve arm

A small ironing board used for pressing sleeves.

Sleeve head

The top point of a sleeve that meets the shoulder point in an armhole.

Snap tape

Another name for popper tape.

Snips

Small scissors or spring-loaded blades used to cut threads.

Speed limiter

A control on some computerised sewing machines used to limit the maximum speed of a sewing machine motor.

Spoons

A term coined by Christine Miserandino to describe how people dealing with chronic pain, neurodivergence or mental health challenges have a limited amount of physical and mental energy to get through the day. Search "Spoon Theory" for more information.

Spring-loaded scissors

Types of scissors that have a spring action built in, making them self-opening.

Stitch length
The length of a sewing machine stitch – basically, the distance between a needle exiting and re-entering a fabric whilst sewing it.

Stitch ripper
A tool used to undo stitching in the event of an error or the requirement for an alteration.

Stop-start button
A button on some computerised sewing machines used to control the machine motor, without the need for a foot pedal.

Straight pins
A type of sewing pin consisting of a long point with a head at the tip, used to secure fabric together in readiness for cutting out or sewing.

Straight seam
A seam created by using a straight line of stitching.

Straight stitch
The most commonly used construction stitch, consisting of one line of stitches.

Stretch stitch
A type of construction stitch used on a sewing machine specifically with stretch fabrics, which allows the fabric to stretch along the seam lines.

Swedish tissue paper
A form of paper used for adjusting patterns and making up toiles.

Tack
Another word for "baste".

Tailor's chalk
A type of chalk used for traditional fabric marking.

Temporary basting spray
A form of spray-on glue used with fabric to hold patterns and fabrics together temporarily.

Thimble
A metal, plastic or leather cup, which fits over the tips of fingers, to be used when hand sewing to help protect the finger tips.

Thread cutter
Hidden blades built into sewing machines for cutting sewing threads.

Thread cutter button
A feature on some computerised sewing machines, used to cut the threads automatically at the end of sewing.

Tissue fit
The act of fitting a tissue or paper pattern piece on a body to check its fit before cutting out the fabric.

Toile
A mock-up version of a garment that turns a 2D pattern into a 3D pattern so the fit can be checked.

Top stitch
A line of stitching that sits on the top of the fabric and can be seen.

GLOSSARY

Top thread
The thread that feeds down from the top spool on a sewing machine to form the upper thread in the stitching.

Twin needle
A specialised sewing needle that has two points rather than one.

Unpicker
Another name for a stitch ripper.

Woven fabrics
Fabrics created by weaving a warp thread and a weft thread together on a loom.

Wrong side
The side of the fabric not seen on the outside of a finished project.

Zigzag stitch
A form of sewing machine stitch where the needle jumps from left to right to create a zigzag-shaped stitch, traditionally used to prevent edge-fraying, or as a stretch construction stitch.

Zip/zipper
A fastening consisting of metal or plastic interlocking teeth running along fabric tape.

Zipper foot
A type of sewing machine presser foot used for the insertion of zips.

Zipper pull
The tab that is pulled on a zip to open and close the coil.

Zipper tape
The fabric tape either side of the zipper coil used to stitch the zip in place in a garment or other fabric project.